THE AFRICAN IN THE MAKING OF CUBAN ART

This book is a publication of
Diasporic Africa Press

New York | www.dafricapress.com

Library of Congress Control Number: 2024937616

ISBN-13 978-1-937306-80-9 (pbk.: alk paper)
ISBN-13 978-1-937306-81-6 (ebook)

THE AFRICAN IN THE MAKING OF CUBAN ART

BÁRBARO MARTÍNEZ-RUIZ

ORBIS AFRICA | SHORT BOOK SERIES

A TALE OF ART, MORAL PHILOSOPHY AND AFRICAN HERITAGES

The work of artists of African descent has been produced and studied within the institutional apparatus of Western art. This book asks whether it is possible to identify Afro-Cuban art or art created by Afro-descendants outside this institutional framework. Can this art only be studied in terms of Afro-Cuban culture, or is it more appropriate to talk about the art of artists of African descent?

Implying that Afro-Cuban art is simply art created by Afro-descendants was a simplification applied throughout the twentieth century. What happened to African artists before the founding of the Academy of San Alejandro in 1818, when people of Africa created the most visual expressions? Mentioned only when it purports to serve as inspiration for the production of vaguely considered art, artwork created by African-Cuban descendants has been generally intended to assign a specific African-Cuban character to their philosophy and spirituality. Cuban art history discourse has consistently assumed the essence of Afro-Cuban art is somehow rooted in African history, religious sources and ethnographic characteristics. I have seen artists, critics and historians talk about the African symbolism that permeates Cuban art in general and the space of artists of African descent. They often base their argument on unenlightened explanations of the African-Cuban experience. They often confess the artist's love for lines and colors that hypothetically talk about African-influenced art. In addition, an exaggerated description of the artist's passion for symbolism is expressed in form factors such as the conception of visual space. Perhaps specific unconscious motives for an "African character" due to recognizable racial factors have held greater sway than a meaningful effort to identify specific cultural principles related to the visual underpinnings of Afro-Cuban religions.

It is difficult to answer whether Afro-Cuban art exists when the main objective in the discussion is to define a general Cuban national art. "Afro-style" has been a critical concept used throughout the twentieth century to highlight African contributions to the nationalistic approach to Cuban art. How can we generously evaluate an Afro-Cuban art history when its historical and present-day protagonists are not endorsed fully in the national narrative?

I suggest a few points that can help to define an artwork

created by African descendants in Cuba:

1. The work of African-descendant artists is produced within the institutional apparatus of Western art.

2. The content must be rooted in Afro-Cuban cultures or conceived in the Afro-Cuban spirit in order to validate its cultural foundations as well as its philosophy and religions.

3. The Afro-Cuban approach is recognizable not only in ideological and emotional issues, but also in traditional values, aesthetic and conceptual choices: Afro-Cuban style and its traditions.

4. The work is produced in an Afro-Cuban social environment of a particular cultural constellation and influence.

A fundamental concern arose during discussions with scholar Robert Farris Thompson between 1999 and 2004 in which Thompson reflected pessimistically on the lack of attention to central themes in African art and art history. The discipline has appropriated a tradition of thought and is now demonstrating action to transform African exploration, testing how historically Africans thought about the world, forced to live in unimaginable conditions like slavery. Thompson's approach evolved at this crossroads, becoming one of the most relevant intellectual endeavors in taking African ethical philosophies seriously in learning culture and arts education and exploring new methods of African studies. In a 1992 interview for *African Art Magazine*, Robert Farris Thompson points this out:

> Through mambo, African-Atlantic traits became my analytic system, a way of viewing the whole world. And it occurred to me: if I was moved, imagine how it hit Amiri Baraka. In fact, I think one could prove that mambo is a secret engine behind a lot of famous people. Gabriel Garcia Marquez defended it. Carlos Fuentes: mambo crackles through his first novel, and in a marvelous way he virtually uses it against Nietzsche. The Palladium and the mambo world were like a proving ground for many African-Americanists.[1]

Topics such as representation, imagery, symbolic traditions, beauty and taste became part of the theoretical discussion of the so-called African "canon." I incorporated these repetitive themes into our research, condensing them into

---

1 Donald J. Constantino and Robert Farris Thompson. Interview with Robert Farris Thompson. *African Arts*, Oct. 1992, Vol. 25, No. 4, 100th Issue (Oct. 1992), pp. 52–63.

visual qualities, as Thompson suggested. He emphasized the importance of a multisensory approach that highlights the immersive, dynamic, and multimedia aspects of African culture. African art and its diaspora in Cuba require a rethinking of cognitive and experiential methodologies that considers comprehension, auditory, olfactory, and other sensory inputs, as well as experiences of pleasure, desire, fear and time, an approach centering individuality and the identity of material objects. Recognizing African ontology as a "multisensory being" confirms its constant exchange with the environment. It can take responsibility for its attitude towards nature, the manifestations of nature (gods), and human consciousness (ancestors). Thompson articulated Africa's humanistic aspirations towards the environment and those around him, challenging the norms that omit the way in which religious beliefs and systems of divination guide actions.

In general, he did not delve into these issues early in his career, as the priority of initial African art history discourse was to focus on case studies. Later incorporating the above-mentioned issues into a much broader systematic methodological theory, Thompson makes a subtle and essential distinction between teaching Western and African art history:

I think that Renaissance art history, compared to Yoruba art history, is easier. The research will be conducted in an Indo-European language and a historical context lauded since your childhood. You know something about Michelangelo already.

Whereas if you are going to study Turkana bead working, you have to learn Turkana. You have to study patterns in provinces all around that area. You can't just go and read the vestry minutes of the Duomo. You've got to go out there and sweat out the puzzle in the middle of East Africa. Our work is harder. We have to read a double, maybe triple literature. You can' t just read art history. You've got to read anthropology. And you can' t just speak English. You've got to speak Mande-Kan or Creole. You've got to put yourself on the line where race, class, society, and culture intersect and not feel sorry for yourself when at first you fail and fail. As Paula Ben-Amos taught me, hit the witch-bird on the beak and *get on with it.*[2]

In February 2021, Professor David Bindman addressed this topic during a panel discussion at the DuBois Institute at

---

2   Ibid., p. 57.

Harvard University, arguing that textuality to convey rituals and art is strictly limited to religious expressions. Seemingly harmless at first glance, this view inadvertently reveals a deep concern about public perceptions of African art and its diaspora in general, excluding other forms of knowledge production that further explore another area of intellectual creativity central to African cultural foundation. According to Bindman, there is a close connection between social systems of African origin, their visual systems, and religious systems. This link restricts our ability to comprehend alternative interpretations of African art.

To formulate an answer to Bindman's ambiguity requires acknowledging the existence of social space for knowledge production alongside the colonial context. African social and cultural spaces are passively explored by accepting the canonical evolution of the Cuban cultural identity through concepts such as hybridization, creolization, or transculturation. It is important to mention several of these institutions of African origin known as self-liberation societies, such as Cimarrones settlements, Quilombos, Palenques, professional associations (independent militias and gilds), and the formation of various African religions. Is it possible to imagine a coherent narrative of Western culture within art history without recognizing the historical role of religion in the development of art? It is impossible to separate the historical function of religion from the story of the evolution of Western art. The rigid binary of art in opposition to religion was central to the formulation of modern art, above all in the texts of Theodor W. Adorno. What are the possible benefits of enforcing a critical theory strictly conceived as part of the intellectual evolution of Western cultures? What is the point of using Adorno's term "cultural industry" outside European culture without analyzing the unique characteristics of African institutional origins? The most logical answer is to adapt Adorno's argument to the context of African cultures. A second possibility is to propose a counterargument from a particular formulation of African epistemologies.[3]

For example, the Ifá Yoruba divination system considers the issue of the works of art and their institutional nature in three main Odù. "Oyekun Meji" traces the origins of art through the development and mediation of specific media, talking, for instance, about creating a framework of meaning through manipulating substances such as clay to make pottery. The Odù "Ogunda Ofun" and "Ojuani Ofun" develop a clear visual vocabulary through painting and representation of adornment, design and symbols while also formulating a description of reflections instrumental to understanding

---

3   Barry Hallen. Yoruba Moral Epistemology. In Kwasi Wiredu, ed. *A Companion to African Philosophy*, pp. 296–304.

photography.

On the one hand, Adorno believes that the technological aspects of contemporary culture discourage artistic innovation by fostering a passive and politically incompetent (alienated) audience, referring to the entire field of mass media production and the culture that produces both ideas and goods for mass consumption. This argument is important because, in Adorno's view, modernist Avant-garde art seeks to resist homogenization. Cuban scholars such as Fernando Ortiz, Lydia Cabrera and Algerian León have explained the concepts of visual production associated with Afro-Cuban culture through specific artistic ideas of these cultures, though their relationships to African-specific cultures are missing, but there has been little interest in characterizing these works as art rather than as the product of ethnographers and folklorists.

African art has had a relatively limited function in changing the conceptual framework of the discipline of art history until the early twentieth century, a field that drew heavily upon African aesthetics from museum exhibits and private collections. The colonial relations with Africa shaped the contemporary art theory that reflects this particular ideological condition due to the center-periphery dynamic, economic determinism and societal dichotomy of civilized versus savage. Although

Western Avant-garde artists and scholars widely recognized African culture as a source of inspiration that radically changed one aspect of contemporary artwork, the aesthetics and its conceptual underpinnings were not. Rather than being an intellectual contribution and conceptually responsible for transforming current and modern art output, African cultures were understood as the primary aesthetic source. The importance of aesthetic aspects of African art has a lasting impact on our relationshipwith Africa. It informed the approach that led to the development of the study of African art in the early 1960s when African art pioneers Roy Sieber and Robert Farris Thompson reassessed the relationship between African artwork and conceptual specifications within the universal narrative of art history, moving beyond what had historically been studied in the context of popular representations to a more networked approach.

The study of antiquity and the Middle Ages was shaped by the rigid functionalism and authoritarian pictorial regimes that preceded the rise of post-Renaissance modernity. This new reasoning begins with an inductive method that views artistic production as an accumulation of data that can subsequently be sequenced and analyzed, along with an approach that focuses on collecting documentary information about individuals and their behavior. It begins with Georgio Vasari's demanding historical approach to visual art that emphasizes the knowledge and humanism involved in judgment about the quality of the artists and their achievements concerning the impact on their intellectual sphere or artistic activities. Humanism is related to forming judgments about the quality of an artist's work and whether their style, sensibility and form are part of the canon of great works of art. Johann Joachim Winkelmann's cultural theory was a significant development in art historical discourse that paid necessary attention to a systematic approach in which artists and works of art inform and are informed by the related knowledge of their time. This evolutionary narrative of art history assumes that Winkelmann's cultural history is a continuation of Vasari's chronological approach, an assumption that is problematic when extended to non-Western fields of art history.

In his book *Theory for Art History*, Jae Emerling states, "Questions central to art historical discourse concern the ontology and meaning of a work of art, its status as a thing or as an inflection of a preexisting discourse (whether historical, stylistic or political), its reception by an intended or ideal viewer, and the role art plays in society."[4] Emerling's summary of the function and development of art is confined to the context of Western art, where ancient European

---

4   Jae Emerling, *Theory for Art History*, p. xi.

philosophical aspects such as aesthetics in Greek art are seen as starting points for production and discussion, and he suggests ontological concerns for Western art can be problematic in the Cuban artistic context. The word art, in the Cuban context, suffers from the assumption of cultural homogeneity that not only contradicts the historical and cultural diversity that is constantly shaping national culture, but also overvalues Western intellectual heritage in Cuban discourse while underplaying the vital role of African cultures in the development of the language of art.

The second aspect concerns the importance of art in society. All artists and social acknowledgments reviewed in this book focus on artists trained in Western-based art institutions. This choice forces us to indirectly maintain a narrative aligned with dominant Western art history. Instead, I suggest approaches to artistic subjectivities that begin with interrogating a relationship with "Africa" beyond racial tropes, an exercise urgent in nature because it alerts the audience to pay attention to Cuban art's artistic discourse and widen the focus from one that mimics the evolution and substance of Western intellectual production.

The practice of centering Western approaches to artistic production and evaluation is seen in the National Academy of Fine Arts San Alejandro, the implementation of Western-based art curricula by the National Academy of Fine Arts

San Alejandro, founded in 1818, and was continued in the "post-revolution" period through the creation of the National School of Fine Art and the High Institute of Art. These three historical moments will be reflected in works examined in this book, conveying values and artistic tastes that primarily favor Western artistic heritage and techniques. Unfortunately, Cuban arts curricula have so far failed to imaginatively engage othervalue systems rooted in specific African cultures and artistic practices.

Perhaps most disturbing in their omission is that discourses about African culture already exist; art history generally sees these historical engagements with Africa as part of the evolutionary hallmark of Western civilization. Recognition of and engagement with these existing historical discourses is essential for reconstructing new theories about Africa in Cuba and elsewhere across the diaspora. Subtly, this assertion promotes a contrast between two areas of artistic production that characterized Western art culture as dynamic and progressive, and Cuban art (in which the relation to Africa emerged through several Afro-Cuban cultures) was defined as part of folklore and more unstable over time. However, most of the historical discourse of contemporary art is that the traditional notions of aesthetics, beauty, truth, and conceptual experience do evolve when challenged by critical theory and new investigations into the consequences of producing and the consumption of art globally.

Because of the importance of understanding the heritage of African culture in the Americas, it is worth listing important examples of continental African philosophy here. For instance, in Akan culture, the concept of man is a complex formulation: *nipadua* (body), *okra* (life-giving entity, innermost self, individual essence), and *sunsum* (constituting a person's personality, spirit), *nkrabea* (personal destiny, embodiment of the future and communicator), *Onyame* (spark of the human supreme being).[5] The Yoruba Ifá divination system presents an essential epistemological question in many recorded texts (*odù/odun*) and oral accounts over the centuries.[6] According to Yoruba high priest and scholar Wande Abimbola, the primary concern of Ifá epistemology is to use the divine wisdom of Ifá to repair the world and teach the human principles of life and cosmogony.[7]

Kongo ontology is another example of African philosophy that has a prolonged effect in the Americas and Cuba. Although Kongo has been among the most studied African civilizations,

---

5 Kwame Gyekye, *The Relation of Ōkra (Soul) and Homan (Body): An Akan Conception*, pp. 59–66. See Emmanuel Chukwudi Eze, ed. *African Philosophy: An Anthology.* Malden: Blackwell. 2005.

6 Olúfémi Táíwò. *Ifá: An Account of a Divination System and Some Concluding Epistemological Question*, pp. 304–311.

7 Ibid., p. 309.

its philosophy has yet to be reviewed or fully interpreted. The Kongo epistemology does base artistic practices on the notion of seeing and activating social mechanisms, making it feasible for humans to create and convey expertise through image-making and art processes. Typically, art processes involve performing art in a manner that facilitates adaptive techniques of rendering in response to new environments and people, colonial domination, the forced dislocation of slavery, and changing monetary, cultural, moral, and non-secular paradigms. Image expression in the Kongo subculture makes statements about relationships among human beings, their environment (marking and describing geographical features), their relationship with nature (seasonal moves and migration), and people and monetary mechanisms. Kongo image writing uses a rich array of cosmograms—the smallest symbolic unit capable of articulating complex stories, moral philosophy, and non-secular principles.[8]

Cosmograms summarize graphically represented symbols that can tell stories of cultural formation and appear at many

---

8   Introduction by J. M. Janzen. In A. Fu-Kiau kia Bunseki Lumanisa, *N'kongo ye Nza Yakun'zungidila. Le Mukongo et le Monde qui l'Entourait*, Zamenga Batukezanga. (Kinshasa: Office Nationale de la Recherche et de Développement, 1969), pp. 3–8. See A. Fu-Kiau kia Bunseki Lumanisa, *N'kongo ye Nza Yakun'zungidila. Le Mukongo et le Monde qui l'Entourait*, Zamenga Batukezanga, (Kinshasa: Office Nationale de la Recherche et de Développement, 1969).

previously documented coastal sites and various artistic and religious objects throughout Central Africa. It has been characterized and continues to be used in everyday settings among numerous cultural groups along migration routes. In each case, many familiar aesthetic and design features, as well as a broad conceptual continuity are evident. Identifying the details of interpretation within each historical and cultural context becomes an integral part of exploring the meaning of art.

After more than four centuries since the beginning of the slave trade that forced Africans to move to Cuba, now is the time to envision the art and artistic practices of African origin in Cuba. Three areas of study are critical to understanding the African artistic tradition and its critical framework. First, clarifying the understanding of art and its aesthetic underpinnings in their intellectual traditions in oral and literary accounts. Second is recognizing the art object's content, which focuses on what it stands for rather than itsrepresentation. Third, understanding the efficiency of artistic objects and their institutional aspects and African institutions, including fraternities, temples, initiatory societies, and religious orders, in conversation with Western cultural institutions such as fine art academies.

Through this book, which explores the various roles of

African descent in Cuban art history, I try to clarify a definition of Cuban art produced by African descendants. Despite some political positions from critics and researchers, such a convenient definition has yet to be available in current academic production. Instead, speculation about the nature of Afro-Cuban art returns to the fact that there is a lot of literature in all Afro-Cuban cultures. Artists producing work for a professional audience around them draw on the institutional frameworks and principles of African culture that each of today's Afro-Cuban cultures represents.

It is appropriate to acknowledge cosmological thinking as an example embodied in the Kongo moral philosophy and it would be helpful to outline a theory of Cuban art that takes the same into account. For instance, in Kongo, moral philosophy, or *Makukwa ma tatu ma lambila Ne Kongo*, expresses Kongo's central ideas through a distinctive emphasis on aesthetics in three-dimensional material depictions. Material representation of three essential elements characterizes Kongo aesthetic principles, as shown walking through the following example:

A. Visual Syntagma: A graphic entity consisting of a set of representations (three-dimensional graphic representations, signs, symbols, ideograms, symbolic characters, words, or phrases) in sequential relation to each other. The cauldron first represents a central idea related to the concept ofthe fire-cooking argument of Kongo cosmological thought. The cauldron is the object-subject meaning of the concept of the microcosm as the physical world run by beings (*kimpungu, isimbi, bakulu*) and phenomena (nature). Second, the cauldron claimed that the living world is constantly transformed by the action of a medium (boiling fire).

B. Fractal Design: A design is determined by the creative iteration of a fractal character (repetition of the same ideas through different visual languages) or cauldron as the central graphic element. The cauldron, symbolic of knowledge, spirituality, and culture, is repeated at the top of the composition in a reduced form. It conceptually suggests a tension in meaning between the resizing of inputs, which means a visual transition from large to small, and the relationship between two types of rendered cauldrons. The main design cauldron represents the macrocosm as a metaphor for the whole world, known as *futu*, in contrast to the more miniature cauldron, which stands for the microworld that defines the social context of Kongo culture, known as *nsi*.

C. Multilingual Expression: The cauldron lid is beautifully engraved, with its three lines bordering the center of the

Figure 1. *Makukwa matatu ma lambila Ne Kongo.* From Marc Felix Coll. Photograph by Bárbaro Martínez-Ruiz, 2000.

cauldron.[9] The three-line design starts from the of the lip to the edge, creating three spaces or compartments. The same principle of the three lines associated with "three

9 See Clémentine M. Faïk Nzuji. *Tracing Memory*, p. 40. Faïk-Nzuji conceptually connects familiar graphic depictions that appear in several initiations among Kongo and neighbor cultures in Angola and the Democratic Republic of Congo. These graphic motifs varied from three dots, three lines or lines, a triangle and the Lemba crossroad:

talking stones" is again represented simultaneously as a graphic motif and a three-dimensional representation by its three stones supporting a small cauldron.

Kongo epistemology suggests that the understanding of "natural limits" could be equivalent to the cultural and symbolic space. The proverb and its visual representation, "three talking stones," articulate the physical boundaries of the culture and simultaneously serve as a metaphor for a common origin connected to a fictitious physical location known as the *ma kisi nsi*. The concept of "stone" articulates the ideas of ethnogenesis associated with three historical founders of the distant past: the origin story, the sense of belonging to a shared history, and the essential moral values that gave birth to Kongo society. Fire-cooking as a family or family formation is recorded in the following fragment of a short story (*savu*), known as *Muna vanga a vata, bafwete lunga a kanda a mvimba*, about creating a commune (*vata*), as told by the late Congolese scholar and religious practitioner Andele Fu-Kiau Bunseki (see figure 1).

Le processus de préparation du fufu (luku), depuis la culture du manioc jusqu'à la farine est long et exige beaucoup de patience de celui qui a cultivé du manioc, s'il veut en obtenir du fufu. Dans l'idée des bakongo l'histoire de l'origine du monde est un processus TRES LONG. Le monde, l'univers est le fufu préparé par Dieu pour se rassasier. Nous voyons aussi une autre idée: du luku conservé pendant longtemps, sort de l'eau et des fentes apparaissent; cela est la cause principale de l'origine et de l'existence de l'eau et des riviéres sur la terre. Dieu, après avoir préparé le fufu, pensa beaucoup trouver de la viande qui convint mieux et suffisamment. Il voulut créer l'homme. Comme Dieu devait attendre la multiplication dugenre humain, le fufu commença à se REFROIDIR, à produire de l'eau et à se fendre. Il en résulta, (après le refroidissement, la sortie d'eau, la formation des fentes, certains endroits déprimés d'autres bombés) des plaines, des rivières et des montagnes; ce fufu avarié devint du fumier pour les plantes qui poussèrent.

The process of preparing fufu (luku), from the cultivation of cassava to the flour, is a long one and requires a great deal of patience on the part of the cassava grower, if he wants to obtain fufu. For the Bakongo, the story of the origin of the world is a VERY LONG process. The world, the universe, is the fufu prepared by God to satiate himself. We also see another idea: from the long-preserved luku, water emerges and cracks appear; this is the main cause of the origin and existence of water and rivers on earth. God, having prepared the fufu, thought very much of finding meat that was more suitable and sufficient. He wanted to create man. As God had to wait for the human genus to multiply, the fufu began to

COOL, produce water and split. The result (after the cooling, the outflow of water, the formation of cracks, some depressed and others bulging) was plains, rivers and mountains; this spoiled fufu became manure for the plants that grew.[10]

Figures 2 and 3, known as "maternity" or "Mother and Child," can be associated with Kongo cosmogram through the portrayal of their body language. For example, the mother figure, by sitting cross-legged, makes a circle with her legs. This pose is called *sembuka*, and it is the position in which one can attract vital forces (energy). Her crossed legs also form *funda nkata*, meaning life's circle of protection or the safeguarding of a child's life. The woman holds the body of the child, forming another circle. A third circle is formed by the decoration on the woman's shoulder. Together these three circles suggest a spiral around the figure that represents multiples level of protection.

Another important element is the imaginary axis suggested by the pose, which bisects the figure from the feet to the head and represents motion from the natural world to the cosmos. This "time axis," or *mukula*, is physically represented by a

---

10 A. Fu-Kiau kia Bunseki Lumanisa, *N'kongo ye Nza Yakun'zungidila. Le Mukongo et le Monde qui l'Entourait*, Zamenga Batukezanga, (Kinshasa: Office Nationale de la Recherche et de Développement, 1969), p. 110. English translation is mine.

Figures 2 and 3. Maternity figure, late nineteenth century to early twentieth century. Democratic Republic of the Congo, Kongo. Wood, copper alloy, and glass. Richard H. Scheller Collection. Photo © Robert A. Kato.

line incised and now cracked down the center of the figure's back. The piece has been designed to draw the viewer's glance upward in a spiraling direction from the mother's left foot through the baby's body, and the woman's arms to the top of her head. This prescribed visual movement creates in three-dimensional and anthropomorphic forms the Kongo spiral or shell, which represents eternal life and the journey between the world of the living and the ancestors.[11]

Figure 4 is a rare example of an *Mpungu* that contains two empowering techniques common in Central African religious practices: the piercing of the upper torso and the knotting of the lower torso. Piercing techniques, employed here on the upper body, are used as part of a process of recording within *mpungu* religious activities such as wishes, desires, protective actions, defense tactics and empowerment. Knotting techniques are generally referred to as *mazita*, the Kikongo term for the act of tying up, and as used here on the lower part of the *mpungu*, clearly illustrate their use as a power signifier. The *mpungu a nkisi* (more commonly referred to in existing literature as *Nkisi Nkondi*) here shows five of the nine basic forms of knotting in the Kongo tradition. For example, the large knot on the figure's base, known as *zita a nkita*, represents the dialectic process of coding and recording through knots, and becomes the unique signature that identifies this *mpungu*. The final visual aesthetic marker that characterizes this *mpungu* is the gesture it is making. Known as *zaka zaka*, or many problems, the gesture aligns both the piercing and the knotting with the vertical design of the head, suggesting the point of entry of vibration into the

---

11 See Bárbaro Martínez-Ruiz. *Embodiments: Masterworks of African Figurative Sculpture*, p. 171.

Figure 4. Dondo-Kamba people. Democratic Republic of Congo. Wood, iron, cane, ritual materials. H 53 cm.

object and the direction in which the figure's energy flows. The figure's sharp teeth, depicted in a zigzag motif, are a sign of protection, further symbolizing the spiritual power of the figure.

The only example of historical African art that survives in Cuba is called "Ídolo Matiabo" (known as "Ídolo de la manigua de Cuba") and was confiscated from Cuban rebel forces during their fight for independence from the Spanish colonial army in the nineteenth century. Images were published as part of a propaganda campaign in the Spanish newspaper *La Ilustración Española* on August 15, 1875 (see figures 5 and 6).[12]

I am deliberately seeking to assess this subject's artistic or cultural value in its historical context. Lydia Cabrera briefly mentions this object in her 1948 book *Porqué: Cuentos Negros de Cuba*, describing it as a puppet figure.[13] The artistic and cultural appreciation of this object is only referenced in two published volumes, in Robert Farris Thompson's 1984 *Flash of the Spirit* and Bárbaro Martínez-Ruiz's 2012 *Kongo Graphic Writing and Other Narrative of the Sign.* [14]Unfortunately, the object has disappeared from Cuban history and is entirely unknown within Cuba's Kongo-based religious community. Farris Thompson's assessment, by comparison, is much closer to developing an African focal-theoretical apparatus for evaluating art.

---

12 La Ilustración Española, Año XIX, No. XXX (15 de Agosto 1875), p. 1.

13 Lydia Cabrera, *Porqué: Cuentos Negros de Cuba.* (Habana: Ediciones C & R, 1948), pp. 248–49. See Robert Farris Thompson, Flash of the Spirit. Pp 124–125 and 286.

14 Robert Farris Thompson. *Flash of the Spirit: African & Afro-American Art & Philosophy.* Random House: Toronto: 1984.

Drawing a theory based on the object's function and social condition, Thompson writes:

> It was strongly Kongo-influenced and came equipped with horn (*mpaka*). *Matiabo* were runaway slave who sometimes joined forces with rebel forces in Cuba's nineteenth-century war of independence against Spain. They probably used such charms—even as human figurines mounted on antelope horns were used in Kongo—to expose sorcerers, heal the sick, and locate game (in Cuba the quarry was approaching Spanish soldiers).[15]

Although the references functioned as Spanish propaganda in the press of the time, they clarified the Spanish prejudices involved in evaluating African material culture. The newspaper publication illustrated the ideological position on artistic value; for example, in the first sentence of the description, the evaluation of the figure of *Matiabo* is evident through the characterization of the ornaments as "ridiculous." Ignoring the specific aesthetic practice in African art of re-valuating an object using materials of high social value like gold, silver, or imported textiles like corduroy, the

15 Ibid. 125.

description dehumanizes the African-based practice of this object and the people who wield it. The post emphasizes the aggressive demeanor of Matiabo, referred to as a receptacle for the cinders of incinerated Spanish soldiers. Furthermore, the author characterizes Matiabo as an "unfamiliar item" divergent from conventional European aesthetics. The author belittles the object by portraying it as a nearly unclothed entity, implying its savage essence. Additionally, the writer questions the artwork's artistic value while describing its unsophisticated, rudimentary sculptural style.

Representa un negro casi desnudo, toscamente esculpido en madera de caoba; sus ojos son dos pedazos de vidrio, y ostenta en la cabeza, por via de ridículos adornos, algunas peonias y varios amuletos de oro; la caja del cuerpo está hueca y servía para encerrar en ella cenizas de cadáveres de españoles quemados por los insurrectos...

Represents an almost naked black, roughly sculpted in mahogany wood; his eyes are two pieces of glass, and he shows on his head, by way of ridiculous decorations, some peonies and various gold amulets; the body box is hollow and served to enclose in it ashes of corpses of

Spaniards burned by the insurgents...[16]

Al apoderarse nuestras tropas del extraño ídolo, un negro prisionero se arrodillo ante el soldado que le había cogido y exclamo llorando: ¡Máteme su mersé, mi amo; pero no toque esa grandeza de losmontes!

As our troops seized the strange idol, a black prisoner knelt before the soldier who had caught him and exclaimed crying: Kill me master, my owner; but don't touch that greatness of the forests![17]

¡Mentira parece tanta superstición, tan bajo y miserable fanatismo!

Lie seems so superstition, so low and miserable fanaticism![18]

Y no solo los negros, sino también (¡vergüenza es decirlo!) los blancos que formaban en la partida insurrecta adoraban al ridículo Matiabo... "

---

16 La Ilustración Española, Año XIX, No. XXX (15 de Agosto 1875), p. 1.

17 Ibid

18 Ibid

> And not only blacks, but also (shame is saying it!) the whites who formed in the insurgent game adored the ridiculous Matiabo.[19]

The most disorienting comment is the reference to the power dynamics between the Spanish soldiers and the Cuban rebels, specifically where the rebels refers to the Spanish soldiers as their master and begs them for mercy. It also is complemented further by a characterization of rebel practice as superstitious and fanatical—ending with a comment on the embarrassment that white rebels also adored this idol. The last two observations open the possibility for a better understanding of Kongo-based practice in Cuba related today to the Palo Monte religion.

Kongo art cannot be limited to a particular medium, style, or subject. What practitioner often characterizes as the Kongo's creation principle is called *vanda*, which means "to do," and is conceptualized before the thing/object is created and crafted. What matters is the source of creative power (*bilongo*: medicine, nature or matter), not the origin of the thing/object. For this reason, the character directly relates to the creative process of presiding over art or creation. The

---

19 Ibid

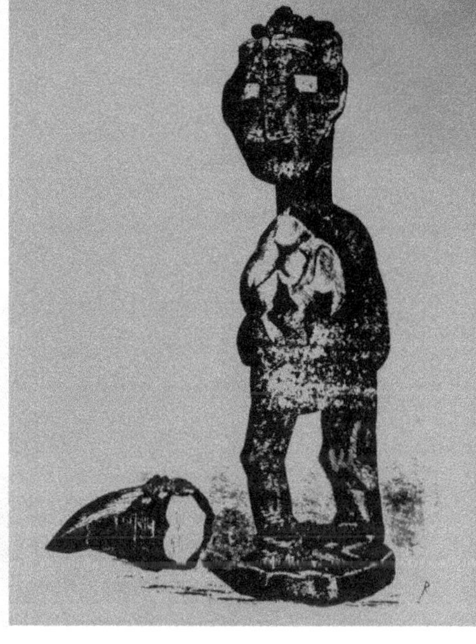

Figure 5. *Ídolo Matiabo*. Before 1875. Cuba. Spanish Military Museum.

Figure 6. Illustration from publications of Lydia Cabrera, Robert Farris Thompson, and Bárbaro Martínez-Ruiz in 1948, 1984 and 2012.

knowledge involved in the organized production of the thing and the result is known as *kubika a bundu,* which means "the art of organizing or gathering." All forms of Kongo art are grounded in a fundamental principle that encompasses an understanding of the natural world as a source of both physical and spiritual resources. This principle assumes a hierarchical system of values and relationships within the specific context of *lusansu lwa Kongo,* or traditional Kongo culture. It also acknowledges a sense of connection to a tangible and material world that can be envisioned mentally, referred to as

Ma kisi Nsi According to several Kongo sources, matter or nature is likely to be complemented by the creative principle that underlies the practice of *Mpungu/Nkisi*, known in Cuba as *Prenda/Ganga*.[20] Generally speaking, Kongo works of art will necessarily meld with some material, designed in principle and animated by spiritual forces. The power inherent in the *Mpungu/Nkisi* form must be equivalent to the embodiment of the vitality of nature and the spiritual world. Likewise, the effect on clients and audiences goes beyond what is physically present and immediately visible.[21]

One of the early documentations of Kongo art is a form of the cauldron that coincides with the most common Kongo prototype or style of art in Cuba. This example demonstrates a continuity of Kongo art in Cuba and as a process of recoding African artistic principles into a new social reality. Coincidentally, the representation of fire as a transforming agent and cooking, as a result, was captured in the illustration of the Capuchin monk Giovanni Antonio Cavazzi da Montecuccolo during his stay in the Congo kingdom in the 17th century (see figure 7). In the first instance, this type of visual material had the primary function of informing specific

---

20 Bárbaro Martínez-Ruiz. *Call and Response.* Pp. 79–82.

21 Bárbaro Martínez-Ruiz, *Ma ksi nsi: L'art des habitants de la région de Mbanza Kongo.* Pp. 14–16, and 25–32.

aspects of the culture and habits of populations outside Europe, non-Christians, and thus future candidates for an evangelization process. There is a possible second interpretation of these images, one more related to the ability to understand the subject under study through the prism and from the ideological point of view of the Catholic Church.

Figure 7. Illustration that shows an early representation of a pottery N'kisi, known *as a prenda* in Cuba's Palo Monte religion, from Giovanni Antonio Cavazzi da Montecuccolo, *Descrição Histórica dos Três Reinos do Congo, Matamba e Angola, 1687.*

What is remarkable in this image is its ambiguous nature regarding what and how it is represented. It is noteworthy that the artistic principles of Kongo are not echoed in Cavazzi's artistic interpretation and explanation of a Kongo cultural event known as a "rain call." Above all, it is a simplification of the three-dimensional visualization in figure 1, reducing it to a bi-dimensional representation typically seen in prints, maps, and travel narratives of this time. Cavazzi does not offer any written comment about the fact of the "rain calling" ritual or its validity as a phenomenon to induce rain through religious practice, positioning himself more like an accidental ethnographer in constructing the image. Cavazzi collides multiple temporalities of the same religious performance by representing symbolic actions such as fire, smoke, rain rays, body gestures, and blowing drink into the open space.

Cavazzi explains his unawareness or inability to fully understand the premise of the religious performances in the main text that accompanied the image. He specifies that he could not translate the experience of the ritual into his language. He chose instead to use concrete visual resources, such as the symbolic representation of a cauldron as a power resource capable of transforming physical reality—the use of fire as a metaphor for action that represents the transformative capacity of the cauldron. Finally, the upper part of the image concludes with rain, represented by the rays or diagonal lines across the sky. All this is happening simultaneously in the same visual frame: creating the rain, manipulating nature, and realizing rain as a natural phenomenon. I concluded that Cavazzi indirectly and naively described aspects of Kongo cosmogony and parts of its religious system. Three key implications were detailed in a complementary relationship between a descriptive text and the image: image and text as completing each other, what the text could not explain could well be understood in the image and vice versa. Symbolically, the complementary relationship between text and image implies the ability to collectively manipulate the physical world and revere nature as a transformative entity. The text's depiction of the activation process is complemented by the symbolic depiction of fire as an activating agent, ultimately resulting in the manifestation of rain.

The challenge for Cuban art history is how to characterize an art expression whose fundamental conceptual nature is considered a living being (see figure 8). It is essential to emphasize, on the one hand, that the Kongo tradition in Cuba obeys another visual regime and logic in addition to the iconoclasm imposed by the colonial religious institution on African artistic practices. What is known as "iconodule" is an attitude founded on restricting ideological usage toward image production and only for aesthetic contemplation. Secondly, the arts of African origin were violently disputed due to the acculturation process charged by the colonial institution that condemned the production of African religious images and their consumption and denunciation as idols. The reverence and devotion of religious archetypes and holy figures were prevalent in colonial times. Such practices included paintings of Jesus Christ, wooden saints in churches, images of virgins and apostles in public processions, and worship in sanctuaries.

The terms "transculturation" and "syncretism," as used by Fernando Ortiz, relate to the social disparity between colonial and historical African cultures and the assessment of African production. They also reflect ideological issues and questions around the legitimacy of an art form that deviates from colonial norms. These two concepts work only in one direction, with the inverse transformation strategy prioritizing the value system imposed by the colonial hegemonic logic, often called the "strategy of survival and continuity." In other words, the linguistic and conceptual framework surrounding the discussion of African culture in Cuba through these two concepts is more ideological than cultural or aesthetic.

The educated classes in ancient Europe associated the worship of idols or idolatry with primitive superstitions that characterized the crude and illiterate. The confiscation of the so-called Matiabo Idol in 1875 shaped the general attitudes of the colonial society towards material culture and artistic production of African origin. Matiabo's idol was an object of devotion and reflects the contradictions regarding African art, a comfortable confusion between understanding the origin of idols and icons and the nature of African evaluative art. Historical prejudices against these objects impede the possibility of appreciating African art as the only true expression of African divinity. The associated negative judgments in turn promote the assumption that African idols/icons are misleading objects inhabited by cruelty and evil spirits.

People of African descent could not dispute the purpose of their image production during the colonial era and were even less able to challenge assumptions that images are vehicles for validating knowledge and expression through art. It is essential to emphasize the need for more cultural space to discuss this topic not purely theoretically but more specifically on the nature of the practice of African image production and its intellectual foundation. The other issue here concerns the assumption that the problem of the image as a vehicle of truth described as universal extends to African cultural practices and is separate from the actual application orartistic tradition.

The following two examples are framed as primitive by using the so-called naïve element similar to pictorial examples

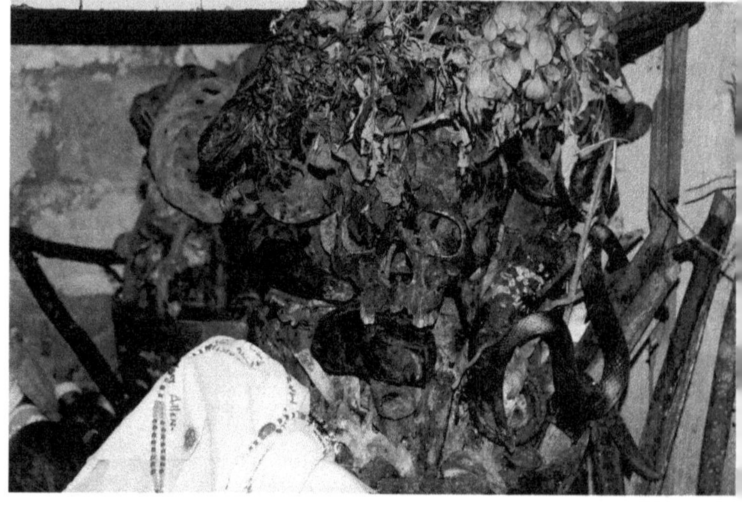

Figure 8. *Sarabanda* represents the vitality that guarantees the generative power of the world. Also known in Cuba as Prenda or Ganga. Interior view of the late Kongo Priest Osvaldo Fresneda Bachiller religious house. Havana 2012.

found in popular paintings (see figure 9). Naïve, in the case of Cuban artists, has its roots mainly in the tradition of European craft, for instance, as a consequence of most of the craft-making, painting, sculpture, and other visual practices being conducted almost entirely by an enslaved person or Afro-descendant until the formation the San Alejandro Academy in 1818. Rare "folklore art" was seldom abstract; it practically always used a figurative visual style. This was the result of needing to be able to translate from the Kongo religion and philosophy simple messages that conceal from nonreligious audiences specific Kongo religious principles. This style of referring to the intimacy of the spiritual experience is manifest in these two examples: an anonymous painting to be

Figure 9. Anonymous painter. José Bedia personal collection. Miami, 2022.

consumed in botanical houses and a work by a professional artist trained in the Western tradition and initiated in the Kongo religion like José Bedia. Both examples are references to the *nganga/prenda,* known as the object of devotion, the *nso a nkisi* (temple), the place of ritual practice. They rely upon specific symbolism to convey meaning.

The cauldron rendered as a quasi-abstract motif by José Bedia is not only symbolic of Kongo artistic practice, but also functions as a symbol of Kongo religious practice and experience. The double visual game that suggests a certain intimacy as a practitioner simultaneously recodes his spiritual experience for a new type of audience, proposing a new conceptual paradigm for those who could only have access to the cultural and empirical meaning of being initiated into the religion.

The piece is constructed following two principles. the first, symbolic; the second by creating a narrative of lyrical quality within the cauldron as a visual element that supports the humanistic experience Bedia tries to share with his audience.

Figure 10. José Bedia. 'Nkili, Fiongo, Mbela, Chamba, Malafo, Mbúa', 1999.

The symbolic space creates various forms of representation through ideograms, pictograms, and symbols that mainly facilitate a generic understanding of the religious practice. The lyrical narrative is made up of reimagination through an ideological language of material factors that constitute the Kongo religious object. The spiritual practice for Bedia requires a complete understanding of processes and rituals, such as animal sacrifice, worship of God, manipulation of forces, interaction with the spirit of the dead, vitalities of flora and fauna, and cosmic symbols, as an integral representation of Kongo religious consciousness.

Engaging African cultures and their theoretical paradigms as expressed in the diaspora could prove invaluable to shaping a new conceptual framework and political reorientation of the discipline of African art history by promoting a more inclusive, democratic, and ethically sound theory of knowledge. Considering several African intellectual traditions and knowledge productions as critical theories will reveal other possibilities for studying and interpreting the role of African art, culture, and its histories. It will also help to inform a new framework through which it will make possible not only to criticize Cuban art's long engagement with Western art but to rethink the premises of art history at the constant crossroad with Africa.

They are challenging the African phobia within the discipline of art history that seems stuck in specific ways of viewing the world and has historically refused to learn from other art historical traditions. Generally speaking, we regard the Western critical theory as the most valuable foundation of the art history discipline, which still guards the criteria for a viable artistic view, deemed the most objective measurement of artistic truth. Contemporary studies on African modernism, African Avant-garde, African pessimism, and Afro-futurism dominate the art critique landscape on both sides of the Atlantic. Trying to understand those traditions by excluding the epistemologies of belief systems, which incorporate immaterial modes of perception in their knowledge and philosophical pursuits, reduces them to the categories comfortable with Western art. The early recognition of the value of African epistemology begins with Robert Farris Thompson's scholarship that formulates African artistic principles in the visual culture and artistic practice as an emancipated form of life. Thompson further notes that African religious systems would release Africans and African descendants from being embodied only as political creatures dependent on social exchange, moral responsibility and economic conditions, enabling Africans to recognize their historical, social and material existence as an equal form of responsibility for living beings.

The question is to what extent Thompson was committed to defining the central issue in terms of themes not necessarily compatible with the study of African art. Given that African art first emerged in dialogue with other disciplines, such as archaeology, anthropology, linguistics, and critical theory, it stands in contrast to the theoretical currents of Western art. Throughout Thompson's career, we see specific emphasis on critical issues, issues borne from experience with African customs in the diaspora in constant self-reflection with their counterparts in the continent of Africa. The space for the study of African historical traditions, including the African diaspora that Thompson calls "Afro-Atlantic," is noticeable from its first publications in the 1960s to the most recent and offers the personal counterpart that says:

Yes, I *am* political if it is a political statement to say that African-Atlantic culture is fully self-possessed, an alternative classical tradition; that one studies Mbanza Kongo, Ile-Ife, and Kángaba as one might study Carthage, Jerusalem, Rome, and Athens. But I'm saying more than that. *I'm saying that it is just as good.* I'm also saying, since it constantly comes back to what is the vernacular answer, in my study of mambo I came across a text built around the life of a Puerto Rican in New York, Benjy López, whom I would call a mambo man. And what *is* a mambo man, and what is a mambo woman, but a person who lives in a cultural bouillabaisse, who learns from being buffeted by pressures white, black, and brown—how to deal, how to find the radium, as Madame Curie did. Benjy López learned from being up against the max in Anglo-Saxon New York City, as a *boricua* [Puerto Rican] learns how to deal. And how do you deal? By *'feeling inferior to no one, but feeling superior to no one either.' Qué ecuación, mano!*[22]

Thompson's extraordinary power model is advantageous for articulating and interpreting specific traits in African artistic practices. The scholar Alejandro de la Fuente echoes this approach by promoting an Afro–Latino American creative vision as a sensitive manifestation of social ideas, as a participant of the social, moral, political and religious life (colonial condition, slavery, race, and identity). Both scholars recognized the agency of African people and African descendants in the Americas. They also avoid studying African societies in the diaspora within the idea of "nation formation" commonly used by two other diaspora cultures, Irish and Jewish, shifting instead to the concept of specific African cultural group continuity. The notion of a cultural group move awaits a well-known trope under anthropological studies, an ethnic group that does not consider other aspects

---

22 Donald J. Constantino and Robert Farris Thompson. Interview with Robert Farris Thompson. *African Arts*, Oct. 1992, Vol. 25, No. 4, 100th Issue (Oct. 1992), p. 59.

of human experience and creativity. Thompson's scholarship pays particular attention to what he thought were the cultural groups in Africa that contribute the most to the Afro-Americas, including the Mande, Ewe-Fon, Yoruba Efik, Ejagham, and Kongo, recognizing the so-called "African traditions" as historical cultures, with linguistic diversity and valid intellectual projects.

Thompson's positivism has, unfortunately, been understood to assert and essentialize Africa. However, his scholarship allows us to understand concrete forms of reaction to colonialism and the social structures to which millions of Africans were subjected for more than five hundred years through the practice of slavery and racist policies. He outlines a new power system that subverts, destroys, appropriates, and replaces the obstacles imposed by a colonial project. It is a pragmatic approach that counters the so-called Afro-pessimism that prevents our imagining that there is an alternative to the colonial totalizing project, a colonial project that clearly understood the systemic benefits of a vertical power structure that justified the practice of slavery, a design whose central objective was the reconstruction of imperial infrastructures in Europe. The imposition of a government system that preached about the African subject's inefficiency and inability to understand systems, development and progress went hand in hand with the historical conception of Africa as an economic zone that produced the goods necessary to guarantee the industrialization of Europe and remains a provider and producer of natural resources then consumed elsewhere.

It proposed an innovative approach that legitimized Africans' knowledge systems that transcended the unimaginable conditions of slavery. Africans could continue an intellectual project despite the historical and present-day impediments, precisely because of the manifestations of African cultures and cultural and religious institutions that incorporated the linguistic impact of colonial languages imposed on African populations in the Americas. It placed a focus on what was unintentionally beneficial to African people in a new social context and argued for a comprehensive study of how Africans conceived new instruments and socially organized their communities on their own terms. Where the notion of self-development and self-power was fundamental, the research should focus on the formation of African cultures and on becoming African today.

SALVATION FROM ANGUISH: NOTES ON AFRICAN AND AFRO LATINO AMERICAN ART

African historiography needs to recognize the distinction between history and culture. The study of human affairs and the manifestation of visual achievements in the current scholarship model incorporate methodologies from anthropology, art history, history, and visual culture studies, overlapping and inseparably merging together.

Current historical and visual studies are dominated by the belief in a single religious proficiency (Catholicism) of Kongo enslaved people transplanted from Central Africa during the transatlantic slave trade. It is important to recognize the power imbalance inherent in such a study. In general, cultural study scholarship asks innovative questions and reveals diverse possibilities for studying and interpreting culture and its histories. In the specific Kongo context, this would involve various critical factors such as emphasis on language subjectivity, politics (racial, gender or sexuality) and other forms of religious traditions in Africa. These views lead to a complete assumption and familiarity of a single religious experience without fully addressing the notion of religious diversity and continuity of Kongo descendants in the diaspora.

I recommend that an independent African religious process in Africa and the diaspora be distinguished from the parallel process known as syncretism and transculturation, in which, over the last five centuries, African people and their descendants have undergone profound intellectual and societal changes. The current study of Kongo culture believes in dynamic processes such as recognition of a core cultural foundation and posits that continuity of Kongo religious principles on both sides of the Atlantic should be considered one of its salient manifestations. As far as African culture is concerned, nothing reveals the intrinsic dialectic of this process more clearly than the fact that the most explicit reassurance of African religious principles is in the present rejection of historical African religion. For example, the Angolan government implemented over decades a systemic ban on religious practices characterized by scrutiny, prosecution and imposition of expensive fees on historical religious leaders known under the term *Ma kisi nsi*, for example religious organizations such as Bunda dia Kongo,

Mpeve a Nlongo, and Botanical House of Mbanza Kongo. Although the theme of social prejudice is similar, it is worth emphasizing the contrast with the African diaspora, where we witnessed the revival of African religions.

Some of the paradigmatic writing on Kongo history denies the authority and foundation of Kongo culture by casting doubt on its core principles and questioning attempts at constituting a Kongo ontology from the time of slavery to the present day. It may be helpful to glance briefly at the question of creolization as a critical notion in contemporary cultural studies and to hear what they had to say on the common subject. John Thornton's book *Africa and Africans in the Making of the Atlantic World, 1400 – 1800* had a profound impact on current scholarship. What constituted a historical fact for Thornton, who focuses mainly on the authority of Western primary sources in constructing a historical narrative without full recognition of the historical fact, and in what kind of media does this historical narrative operate? For instance, Thornton does not look to sources such as the legal account recorded through a lyric in the Lumbu paramount court, the indigenous graphic writing systems like Mandombe script or rock painting visual narratives. What is the nature of image production from Western written sources and ideological production? The general argument that attempts to develop a systematic explanation of the social and political universes without drawing on specific artistic and visual traditions. He also undermines his authority in understanding historical matters by presuming and presenting as fact that all Africans recognized Catholicism one way or another. We should problematize the very principle and lead new viewers out of the "sole religious model" by showing the fundamentals of new scholarship beyond what we understood as "historical fact."

Along with what the new type of knowledge production, such as art and material culture, may have to say regarding artistic sensibility, we must ask how Kongo people qualify their experience aesthetically. What is the nature of art play in the formation of a Kongo ontology? The relation between Kongo ethics and aesthetics is the validity of political and social response to hegemonic power instead of conceiving visual expression to exchange its appreciative role. In other words, its role in African society and how it is appreciated generally affects their community and those outside it. The aesthetic ideas and artistic theory of African art and its diaspora go to the heart of the development of art history as a discipline. It is not, therefore, merely a history of the discipline, but a fundamental question about the definition of art and an invitation

to a reorientation of the field in the context of conceptual, ethical and political premises.

Reflecting the growing importance of the African diaspora in the Americas, there is an argument to be made for the merger of the two contested fields, "African art" and "African diaspora." The argument for a combined field explicitly devoted to promoting and sponsoring research on Africa and integrating their histories and experiences into larger analytical frameworks encompassing its counterpart in the Americas is strong, as is the need for readers to consider the sufficiency of existing discourse on the intersection of historical African art, contemporary African and African diaspora current artistic productions, and whether, in light of the complex interrelationship between Western culture and Africa, critical theory adequately incorporates concerns regarding the nature of being, producing, viewing or otherwise consuming art and meaning, and its holistic role in society.

When intellectual discourses approach art in the context of Africa and its diaspora, we accept a category given to us and a default position of the interdependency of notions constructed to explain Western cultural and intellectual heritage. We borrow all the concepts and critical apparatus and follow all fashions enthusiastically. We can, however, subvert the one-directionality of knowledge production by using and tearing down from within the hegemony of knowledge that compromises our mental habits. Echoing the discourse of difference, we can claim a unique ontology and harness the sense of crisis borne of the tension between the ambiguity afforded by being on the periphery and the desire to be part of the "central" Western cultural regime.

AFRICAN HISTORICAL REFERENCES

The challenge of merging "African art" and "African diaspora" should be considered essential to construct knowledge and subjectivity within the notion of African art and the implications for African diaspora art. Retaining Africa as the qualifier for the merged fields will help to integrate otherwise isolated intellectual traditions that recognize the importance of African culture in culturally recognizable territories such as Latin America, the Caribbean, and the United States. Two strands help to define the parameters of what is being called African art. First is the search for a philosophical tradition and thinking rooted in "African" epistemology by translating Western approaches in philosophy.

It is imperative, therefore, to devise an interpretive approach incorporating African indigenous customs and languages, thereby characterizing the African subject matter concerning its cultural, ethnic, and historical associations with the African continent. In so doing one repudiates all manifestations of European colonialism, political supremacy, and ethical domination. Africans have used all political sources of counter-colonialism and imperialism to place the culture of difference as a moralizing principle in the context of Africa's ideology, an ideology that rejects hegemony in the realms of politics, culture, knowledge, race, and the morality that produced them.

The second strand has its roots in political anti-colonial and ideological tendencies such as freedom fighters and the transformation of those into political leaders such as Nigerians Nnamdi Azikiwe and Obafemi Awolowo, Tanzanian Julius Nyerere, Senegalese Leopold Sedar Senghor, Kenyan Oginga Odinga, and Ghanaian Kwame Nkrumah. These discourses were characterized by defending the African human subject and the ethics of self (African) constructed through a new form of subjectivity as independent, postcolonial and "modern" social institutions.

I may say that these two strands facilitated the construction of the history of "Africanphilosophy," specifically as applied in the work of philologists, linguists and sociologists. Such scholars with a robust Pan-Africanist view include Theophilus Obenga, G. James, Henry Olela and Martin Bernal. Additionally, Lucinda Keita's works reconstruct a history of African critical thinking by inscribing the ancient Islamic tradition in northern Africa, including medieval states such as Timbuktu, Songhai, The Ghana Empire, and the Sudanic states of Central Africa. The contemporary scholar of Africa considers those examples critical foundations in creating a niche that occupied current African philosophy, which overlooks historical African epistemological traditions in Sub-Saharan Africa prior to European encounters in the fourteenth century. That scholarship relied on Islamic sources and complemented Egyptian and Abyssinian origins highlighted in the works of Claude Summer's translation of Zar'a Ya'eqob (1599-1692) and Anton Wilhelm Amo (c. 1703 – c. 1759), African philosopher from present-day Ghana, who lectured in German universities of Halle and Jena and focused on faults such as intellectual dishonesty, dogmatism and prejudice. Amo's critiques preceded important foundational arguments around improving society, later developed by idealism and romanticism philosophers such as Schiller, Fichte, Schelling, and Hegel.

The three key concepts developed by Amo helps us understand the vital transition from objective truth (universal) to the subjective nature of the truth (individual), consequently providing a new context about the ethics of discourse. His writing debated the intentionality of formal discussion and reasoning, the pursuit of truth, and a relevant and unbiased manner in presenting information and fact. His scholarship outlines fundamental logical notions central to the idealist philosophical school about societal changes. He believed that improving society should not be a precondition for emotional self-awareness, but an ethical choice made by humans in presenting and dealing with the truth. This particular point is relevant because it had later implications in the romantic school of philosophy about issues of freedom of the individual through three interrelated concepts: freedom, creativity and aesthetic experience. The big question here is why Amo's scholarship is relevant as an African reflecting on significant issues of Western philosophy and not on African Akan philosophy, which was a critical component of his cultural imagination. How different is his critical apparatus from other philosophers and African and African diaspora thinkers?

The approach from a contemporary perspective could go beyond what is known by many scholars as the "de-colonizing African episteme" to reclaiming an African critical position. This exercise recognizes the historical relationship between African and European thoughts, including how the former became a critical inquiry during the Enlightenment, visible in the writing of natural historians and philosophers such as David Hume, Immanuel Kant, and G.W.F. Hegel. Hegel in particular speculated on the nature of the African mind when considering the Western category of universality. According to Olúfémi Táíwò, in his essay "Exorcising Hegel's Ghost:

Africa's Challenge to Philosophy," Hegel formulated a notion of African humanity and civilization but refused African knowledge of an absolute Being (God) and cited this as an essential distinction between African and European notions of humanity. Táíwò critiqued Hegel's thought that arises from the fact that they (Africans) are one with their existence, implying that they have not separated themselves from nature. Leaving no room for doubt, Hegel writes further about this purported lack, positing that African people do not have humanity because of the ascent of an absolute being, another and a higher than his Self.

Hegel's writing locates the place of the African human subject and humanity defined in the European assertion of institutionalized religion through the ideas of transcendence and the revelation before submitting in supplication. In this line of thinking, Hegel wrote, "The Negro exhibits the natural man in his completely wild and untamed state." He also suggested that the African people do not possess any divine entity to the revelation of which Philosophy is committed. Essentially Hegel believed in the spiritual inferiority of African people, staging that "Negroes are mired in sorcery, worship of graven images that are easily perishable, and worship of the dead."[23]

Conceptualizing African people as magical, mystical, irrational and therefore inferior, dark, savage and primitive has profound implication for social science and humanities discourses and serves to devalue African epistemological contributions to notions such as culture and art.[24]

In the early twentieth century American diaspora, two critical discourses emerged from a group of intellectuals active during the Harlem Renaissance, such as Alain Locke, Claude McKay, and W.E.B. Du Bois, examining Africa and the African mind as a form of philosophy. Du Bois defended the African identity in the United States by recognizing two necessary assurances, first emphasizing the importance of African culture in the new geography of the diaspora in the American context. Secondly, there was an acknowledgment of an ontological crisis faced by many African Americans explained through the concept known as "double consciousness," which was understood generally as recognizing dual experiences of being both American and

23 See *Olúfémi Táíwò* in http://www.virginia.edu/woodson/courses/aas102%20(spring%20 01)/articles/femi.htm

24 See G.W.F. Hegel. *The Philosophy of History*, trans. J. Sibree, introduction C.J. Friedrich (New York: Dover Publications, 1956). P. 93.

African, in which race signified an intellectual and cultural parity between white and black. A similar type of argument of a single designated philosophy flourished in the African continent, known as "Bantu Philosophy." It was considered a strong value in reconstructing African thinking. In this case Western anthropologists like Leo Frobenius, Melville J. Herskovits, and Maurice Delafosse recognized that African people nursed their own form of civilization before the encounter with Europeans, in so much that Frobenius called the experience of colonialism "African Atlantis."[25]

Historically the interrelated relationship between Africa and its diaspora formulation of a discourse about "art" has a second formulation in late 1920s in the Negritude movement in Paris by Aimé Césaire, Leopold Sedar Senghor and Leon Damas. Negritude formed an organizing principle of African identity manifestation based in an evidenced empiricism and ontology and its subsequent ordering and analysis of the experience of being African through blackness and sublimation of Africa as the solo source of identity, that is, cultural identity associated with a specific geographical space (African continent) and an ideology of counter-discourse to Western hegemony.

25 See Leo Frobenius. *Und Afrika Sprach: Auf den Trümmern des klassischen Atlantis.* Berlin: Vita, 1912.

The emphasis on identity subjectivity reveals other possibilities for studying art that came to fruition in the 1960s and 1980s in the work of intellectuals such as Edouard Glissant, Patrick Chamoiseau, Jean Bernabe, and Raphael Confiant. Those authors rejected the essentialist approach of the Negritude movement, which concerned access and interpreted Africa as only directional and dependency on Africa as the most significant factor in forming an African identity. Antillanité emerged as an act of interpretation concerned with these hidden and visible cultural forces that shaped the Caribbean identity. It was primarily the identification of a new conceptual paradigm, which claimed multiple cultural factors in the formation of an African identity due to the cultural diversity of the Caribbean. Identity is understood through an Antillean discourse as a political trait restricted to recognizing the changes in artistic expressions of an African character in the Caribbean, yet totally disconnected from their counterparts in Africa. In other words, Antillanité pledged to identify the internal development of the Caribbean's multicultural and historical reality and how the relationship between ideas and history shaped the discourse of Caribbean identity.

I intend to problematize two aspects related to the representation of Africans and their cultures in Cuba. The facts are that two parts of historical significance could help to understand the African legacy and contribution to visual language and art in Cuba, physically transported over five centuries. However traumatic and violent the transatlantic slave trade, Africans created a viable life for themselves through several mechanisms that scholar Daniel Dawson called "the self-liberation strategy." This strategy means the Africans in Cuba and elsewhere in Latin America and the Caribbean managed to create an alternative mode of living outside the colonial space known as palenques. Like palenques, "Cabildos de Nación" is another form of negotiation in the social, political, cultural and other ideological manifestations such as religion, faith, creed and spirituality, successfully created and operated as alternative spaces under the Spanish colonial area. Furthermore, Africans learned how to co-exist with other people from Africa and the world diaspora.

I list here some crucial questions and problems to understand Cuban art and culture and the role African cultural heritage played in informing critical conceptual and aesthetic principles. How do artistic regulations defined by Western culture differ from what characterizes Cuban art? It is possible to explain specific artistic principles applicable across Cuban art without overgeneralizing? How does Afro-Cuban art fit into this developing regional narrative? Does Afro-Cuban art need to be defined in opposition to African,

African American, Afro-Caribbean or Afro–Latin American art, or is there space for an integrated narrative? How does African cultural diversity fit into this, and what are the risks of overgeneralizing? How do African paradigms of race or soul prevent a proper examination of how African culture shapes Cuban art? How does the nationalistic impulse trouble the desire for authenticity and identity?

THE PROBLEM WITH GENERALIZATION

Research on the Cuba's formative period as a nation beginning from late fifteenth-century Spanish encounter in 1482, and consequently the implementation of a colonial project, to the end of the second American occupation known as "Cuban Pacification" in 1990 will help us to examine the visual and spatial representations of Cuban space by European and American cartographers and in the written accounts of explorers, travelers, geographers and religious missionaries. The examination of cartography, printmaking and travel book narratives will focus on how such media both draw upon and shape understandings of African culture continuity and the formation of a new paradigm in a new socioeconomic space. However, the approach taken here will be rooted in the economic, social, cultural and political history of the Atlantic empires.

In examining the observation, and ultimately the manipulation, of the cultures encountered in the Caribbean, the preexisting social, cultural and physical realities and organizations therein become visible. The formal discipline of cartography in Europe from the Renaissance through the late nineteenth century bequeathed a wealth of maps that serve as primary records of encounters with a new land. The representational language therein, previously called upon to imagine and document, became a tool by which to demarcate, label and control the unknown. Even as their purpose shifted, early maps of the Caribbean contain a wealth of detail on local building design, use of urban spaces and material culture production, all as initially recorded by Western eyes.

During the same period, continued proliferation within the landscape genre and an upswing in the popularity of printmaking in Europe provided additional avenues for artists to depict scenes of the new world. An excavation of the ideologies and understandings of the "other" in these early representations of the Spanish, British, Dutch and French empires shows how knowledge of (and attitudes toward) foreign visual traits, economics, politics and cultures evolved and demonstrates how a new sense of self emerged, one defined in part by the relation of the self to space, power and imperialism. Focusing on these depictions can inform a contemporary study of cultural and architectural production both as experienced within and as seen from outside. It will also facilitate a renewal of understanding of power and subjectivity in relation to non-Western cultures and could bridge the gap between conservative Africanist and nativist perspectives and further address some of the key assumptions of postcolonial theory.

The act of mapping formed a network of domination and control over both the Africans that were being mapped, and in relation to the other powers likewise seeking to know and own the world. Maps and modes of navigation played a determining role in the relative stature and wealth of European nations from the fifteenth to the nineteenth centuries, a role that further demonstrates their power to define and order.

The discussion of representation and image in cartography starts by first looking at a general map of Africa from the year 1595, as seen in figure 11. This map provides an example of the manner in which Europeans tried to document the physical space of the African continent, and demonstrates the impossibility of truly representing the cultural complexities that exist beyond the map. This initial representation of African space on the part of the European cultures served primarily to appropriate the space of an "other" and demarcate the boundaries of their new possessions.

This map of the African continent with its representational language is close to the contemporary maps of Africa. The

Figure 11. Gerardus Mercator. *Africa ex magna Orbis Terre Descriptione*. c. 1595.

notion of representation in this first moment is within the realistic and formal canons that have defined cartographic style. The reality portrayed is measured by the mathematical precision of the coordinates and geographic locations that are represented in the map. I am able to understand that the map represents, in this case, the geographic reality of Africa as that which could be represented in a photograph of the continent taken from a satellite. The two mediums (cartographic and photographic) are representing the same object within a convention of human-catalogued reality that attributes value to perception and not conceptualization. Understood within

Barthes' methodology, this map contains three types of messages: first, a linguistic code for the utilization of the map as a document for orientation and navigation; second, iconic messages such as the stamp (illuminated symbol on the left side) that represents the European country that developed this project and ordered the geographic forms represented in the space; and lastly, the map as a document that is an object of a political and historical moment that represents a view and a form of reality and conceptualization of the world from the occidental perspective.

This general map represents the desired Africa, and as a representation, we are able to understand it according to the forms of communication of the era, but it doesn't represent the reality of Africa as a physical space. I believe it is clear that the diversity and complexity of Africa at the height of the sixteenth century could not be represented in any artistic medium or form of representation; this map only represents the surface of a "reality" that is much more complex.

When Roland Barthes refers to language as a continuance of the ideas of Ferdinand de Saussure, he announces that "the relation between signified and signifier is quasi tautological," meaning that it auto-defines one to the other simultaneously. How could this relation of reciprocity define in objective (actual) form the object it intends to represent (Africa), or is it that, in reality, it is not trying to represent Africa, but merely its physical coordinates as produced by the illusion and imagination of those in Europe?

Barthes explains the role of photography that characterizes the relationship between signified and signifier as a medium of "recording" or as a medium that mechanically captures the scene, because, as Barthes suggested, the photograph machine guarantees the objectivity of the reality. The objectivity of the reality in the map could be in the order of the representation of the geographic coordinates, but not of the complexity of the "reality" that supposedly must be represented in this map or a photograph. I believe that both mediums represent a type of objectivity limited to portions of life and human experience, but not the representation of that which we understand as reality (mechanical representation close to the conventionality, the reality and conceptualization of perception).

This map, "Africae nova description," printed by Willem Janszoon Blaeu, is an example of European cartography from the Dutch mapmaking school during the golden age, the style of which came to be known as *carte à figures*. This new visual rendering was an attempt to accommodate the new demand for exploratory projects in Africa. This style is a good example of second-generation mapping after almost a century and a

Figure 12. Willem Janszoon Blaeu "Africae nova descriptio." 1644.

half of constant mapping of the African continent that mainly produced general maps depicting the broad outline of the continent, misplacing cultural group, kingdoms and physical features and renaming and rearranging nature. This map is an example of a new visual rendering that aimed to be more specific as a result of more encounters with African people and the flourishing of trade and commerce (see figure 12).

The problem of intentionality with the European gaze and the presentation of Africa is one of consciousness. Interactions between Europeans and Africans forces each to engage with something in worlds beyond their own. The capturing of these encounters as points of reference materializes through the visual language used in maps and the accompanying written caption. These indulge a specific ideology by attending to representations of a people's customs and habits, new spaces and places that become simultaneously the object and the subject.

The map offers aesthetic parameters that allow us to understand the notion of "intentionality" as a form of visual expression. Images unveil conflict with the need to see things as they are, for instance visual statements and evidence of the state of affairs between early (fifteenth century) European explorations and African negotiations of their place in the world. The new approach to "Africa" that allowed Africa to become a "reality" through verbal and visual aids had its moment of greatest apogee during the sixteenth century and depended on five innovative elements:

"General views": a mix of horizontal views of the space from above with predominant outlines of land, island or continents.

"Oval views": continuous panels of mixed landscape views placed as top panels depicting cities and their topographical surroundings, mainly trading ports relevant at the time for trading and commerce.

"Cartouches": side panels depicting people types (Africans) from places visited along the coastline. The panels stabilized specific information through representation and portraiture, suggesting native people, their customs and habits.

"Decorative traits": lines and pictorial details randomly placed of flora and fauna motifs in the general contour of the continent; lines to represent sizeable African kingdoms and their borders, rivers and lakes.

"Re-naming": use of European languages to name new places, following European spelling rules and using such reinvention as a form of imaging the then-unknown interior of the continent.

This map is an example of the result of a perceived encounter and of limited knowledge of Africa. Its indirect attempt at creating a truth allows for imagining and deploys a visual narrative as an artificial and constructed way to have access to the "real" world of Africa. Perceived experiences, intentions, imagination and distress are all merely intended to allow the imaging of African people, culture and resources in the mind of the European image-maker and audience. This intent can only succeed if the visual language succeeds, if the conceptual premises are competent enough to satisfy a seemingly factual illusion of Africa. The content proposed on this map is only possible through the desire to understand Africa, but on the other hand, it has profound implications for creating an uncomfortable, almost embarrassing perception of Africa as a primitive, mindless subject of oddity, a perception that both affects how Africans see themselves and aids in the implementation of the occupational and colonial project of the nineteenth century.

On a broader level, this method of deconstruction and reconstruction, and the details and the cultural knowledge it reveals, helps to demonstrate the manner in which cartography has been used as a powerful form of representation, imaging, and control of the self and of the other. Ontologically, Western art theory has defined the notion of the production of artwork as important from the Renaissance to the present. Precisely in the moment when the European metropolis needed a new medium for the representation of "other" space, artistic cartography emerged as a strategy for symbolic domination. As seen above, the Dutch (and to a large extent, the rest of the European colonial powers) developed an artistic medium that has the function of representing this first moment of recognition and meeting the "other" that, for Michel Foucault, was that outside the borders of modernity.

In addition to artistic representations of control over the other, this period saw a transformation of notions of domination and order from theoretical forms expressed through mapping to the literal European occupation and rule throughout the continent. Africa had been an imagined space and desired territory of the Europeans since they first encountered it, although their initial conquest was impeded for various reasons, including the military technology of African civilizations, geographic factors such as the climate, disease and internal conflicts between the diverse ethnocultural groups' reigns, empires and civilizations (Yoruba, Kongo, Akan, Mande, etc.) that dominated the first moments of two centuries (sixteenth and seventeenth). But by the mid-nineteenth century, African space was nearly completely appropriated by foreign powers, ushering in a period of colonial subjugation and exploitation.

To look further at the concepts of representation and image discussed in relation to this map, I believe it is important to emphasize that Saussure refers in his study of language as natural, but does not apply his work to other spheres of life and human experience such as art. This definition reduces language and marginalizes other forms of message codification systems wherein the goal of all language is to enable communication within social margins. Nelson Goodman, in his article "Language of Art," also relegates the concept of language to a more restricted zone of human experience, defining the concept of fundamental representation within the nature of art (language of art) as an approach to a theory of symbols like that to which he refers when he states, "representations, then are pictures that function in somewhat the sameway as description."

Michael Shapiro, in defining what he terms "symbolic national schemes," classifies them into two types: that which is defined by characterization of determined social classes, local identities or marks pertaining to a select group, society or political group; and second, the legally and geographically defined character of a nation (country). In general, the first is a symptom of the capitalist appetite of European societies, and the second is an example of the imposed portrayal of a culture that is expressed beyond the limitations of the medium and the contradictions of the forms of European domination. The maps examined above represent aspects of cultures that maintain these trails and parallel them in the contemporary culture of the region. As the production of natural language requires two parts — a mode of call and response — the production of pieces of art, including maps, comes from the interaction between a maker, or artist, and an object that becomes the representation.

With its powerful legacy, and the implications it has for anthropology, art history and other disciplines examining cultures, expressive forms and modes of communication and control in Africa, Jan van Kassel's painting echoes the conceptual and aesthetic principles used in the cartographic medium in which the visual representation of Africa in the Caribbean as a subject matter takes a new direction. Depictions of African people are replaced by representing some aspects of African material culture, specifically in this painting by depicting a sculpture.

There is, unfortunately, no way of knowing what van Kassel hoped to accomplish, nor what statement he intended to make regarding power over the "other," or learning about and demystifying that which is beyond Europe. The reference here to African material culture and religious life could open a new line of enquiry around the notions of art or artifact in which the representations themselves could be seen as acknowledging an African continuity of a form of spirituality or religion. Van Kassel proposes an existential question not based on notions of desire and will, but to the contrary, the use of African material culture symbolism could be seen as a suggestion of an existential mobility and a strategic capacity for reconstructing and adapting themselves in a new environment, consequently defining their humanity.

The first images of the Americas in primary sources in which African people appear are in the Theodore de Bry publication

Figure 13. Theodore de Bry. *India Orientali.*, Vol. 10, 1592.

"India Orientali" volume number 10 printed in 1595. During the fifteenth and seventeenth centuries, travel narratives were characterized by a "double referential" between image and text that should be understood in relation to each other in order to achieve the final goal of creating a new reality through visual and verbal meanings. The early cartographic examples developed a form of notation and representation that saw independent image and text as incomplete forms of expression in which each medium needed the other to achieve the general goal of communicating information about a place, space, people or culture. While text intends

Figure 14. Theodore de Bry. *India Orientali.*, Vol. 10, 1592.

to deal with intentionality in relation to the reality of places being explored in the Americas, images utilize visual expressions to indirectly convey truth even in the context of limited knowledge of places, people and cultural encounters (see figures 13 and 14).

De Bry references Africa and its people not as an observation of their cultural heritage or material culture, but instead as a subject of a political commentary and only includes four images in the entire series of fourteen volumes. In figure 13 the plate caption reads, "Blacks (Africans) from Moorish land are sent to the New Island Mine," which suggests that the subjects are from Northern Africa or Turkey, part of a replacement labor force called upon due to the rapid extinction of native populations. This label, however, conflicts with the actual caption that accompanied the original image, where De Bry indicates that the pictured Africans came from the region known as Guinea. Leaving far less open to question, the caption to figure 3 of volume5 reads, "When some blacks (Africans) fail their daily task, they are atrociously punished by their master."

The book refers to other types of production in the Caribbean, such as the sugar industry, in which De Bry predominantly presents Africans as slaves comprising the main labor force. This is among the earliest representations of African people in the visual history of the Caribbean, one that precedes by a substantial margin the Avant-garde inclusion of the African as a subject matter oft cited in art history discourse.

The artistic Avant-garde in Cuba during 1927 limited African subjects to racial profiling and visual representations that vividly communicated the socioeconomic disadvantage of the Afro-Cuban. Representation of Africa and representing people of color in images obey a prescribed regime in which African people are mostly naked—generally, naked women—portrayed as workers in factories or performing hard physical work like cutting sugarcane in the field, hungry, poor, homeless and prostitutes, or public entertainers like dancers, musicians or boxers. If we compare the way in which Africans are represented from De Bry's time until the break of the Avant-garde in the late 1920s in Cuba, the notion of cultural representation has not been addressed with distinctive care, and there have not even been noticeable attempts to embody African culture or artistic expression, with the minor exception of certain limited concessions by artists such as Eduardo Abela, Roberto Diago and Wifredo Lam.

In De Bry the representation of Africans obeyed clear political goals as far as criticism of Spanish colonialism. By providing morally dubious images of brutality, enslavement of Africans and reiterated accounts of the extermination of the native population, this approach amounted to more than pertinent visual aids in order to carry on a moral message that critiqued the core of Spanish occupation and colonization of the Americas and the Caribbean.

Visually, De Bry relied on visual narratives organized around several formal principles such as composition around the two visual axes, the use of registers and macro scenes. First, he organized the composition of two vertical axes, one to the left of the image dominated by the verticality of the architecture that emerges from the side of the image almost as if it were entering the image. The architecture represented here is only a partial image of a building from where the soldiers can visually access the production space. The second axis is dominated by the presence of a hill, in this specific example, the mine itself.

The register used by De Bry allows him to offer a commentary that facilitates the audience's understanding of the power relations in the context of production. Notably, the registers are used as a way to emphatically repeat the same critical message about the immorality of the Spanish colonial project. The register introduces the exploitative dichotomies with heavily armed Spanish soldiers and the figure of a person who clearly suggests that he is in control of the production space as if he owns it. To the right of this register you can see the nude Africans working hard. The second register repeats the same dichotomy to the left, where soldiers are jealously guarding the extraction process in the mine, and a third register is dominated by the presence of the mine as a symbol of the Spanish alienation and brutality.

Finally, De Bry's use of scenes, which I refer here as "macro scenes," almost serves as a preview of two of the most critical innovative features introduced in the seventeenth century by Dutch cartographers. The sense of grouping

Figure 15. Jan van Kassel, The Continent of Africa, 1666.

mainly provides context for criticism, the anti-Spanish and anti-enslavement views conveyed. There are three organized clusters, first creating an imaginary diagonal of the left part of the composition towards the bottom of the image on the right side. These are essential in creating progression through the space, beginning with the figure of the Spaniard sitting on the left margin of the image, followed by a second group of Africans depositing soil on the ground, and finally in the grotto-shaped openings in the mine where people are seen working hard. The image repeats visual tensions in the same way that tension happened in each of the registers. I could say that these images contain sketches and formal elements of urban landscapes to the left of the image and industrial landscapes at the upper right side of the image. Especially, this type of industrial landscape reappears more clearly during the industrial revolution in eighteenth century England.

Figure 15 shows a panel representing the African continent among six of the panels painted by the Dutch artist Van Kassel to illustrate the whole world. A detail in this early representation of African art shows a small, seated sculpture right in front of the figure of a white child. The almost insignificant figure is depicted like it is coming out the shadow of the two "dark" characters of the far right of the front register of the painting. It is the only reference to a specific African material culture, here depicted in the form of a sculpture. There are other attempts to represent Africa as subject matter using the "language of exotic or naïve gaze," in which the representation of race is noticeable as a visual signifier—blackness used as an aesthetic marker of otherness, and the embodiment of people and their humanity through native costumes and poses that highlight "African" fashion styles and specific cultural habits like smoking a pipe, living with a lion and holding a dangerous snake.

This painting follows the same visual principles used in Dutch cartography, *carte à figures*, in this case extending the side panels used in maps as full round panels and replacing the depictions of types of people with those of local flora and fauna. This all-around landscape uses the repetition to insist upon the exclusive features of the African landscape and assert specific distinctions, not in the space, but by way of the unique African fauna. Reiteration here operates in a mnemonic component, with panels echoing the same type of representation in the central view panel. The repeated content shows the interior of the architectural space in the space of two door frames with views into outside spaces, landscapes containing on one side a dark cave with figures performing an exotic ritual emblematic of African "primitive religion." On the other side, there is a second landscape brightly drawing us into open nature in which people and elephants appear domesticated. The contradiction between types of representations suggests the dichotomy between the need to know Africa and the unknown Africa. Art, in this case, functions as a vehicle to reconcile such contradictions and impossibilities.

We can, however, use his document, his object of representation, as a tunnel, an invisible passage to another civilization. With its double role, that of purveyor of the European ideological and theoretical framework, and that of a window into the barest aspects of Kongo life, the map creates an avenue by which to understand not only the cultural values and traditions displayed within it, but the very act of mapping the African continent. Though Benedict Anderson (1991) refers to the slew of maps created in the nineteenth century, his comments on their narrative role is relevant here. "Historical maps [are] designed to demonstrate, in the new cartographic discourse, the antiquity of specific, tightly bounded territorial units. Through chronologically arranged sequences of such maps, a sort of political-biographical narrative of the realmcame into being, sometimes with vast historical depth."[26]

It is also valuable to note future avenues for exploration of this map. Primary among these is an investigation of the manner in which an African urban center is designed, experienced, and portrayed. Within this theme one can consider the artist's use of inside and outside, the drawing of boundaries and the creation of ordered space inside the city walls while traditional activities remain outside. The spatial organization of the image is interesting, with easily represented activities of the "other" dominant in the foreground, while the calm, grid-like, almost modern town lies in the background. A decision was clearly made as to what was a more "accurate" picture of this civilization; one can only wonder on what

---

26 Benedict Anderson. *Imagined Communities.* London: Verso Books, 1983, p. 175.

grounds. On a more literal level, the map holds important, detailed information as to the architectural style of the Kongo civilization at this point in history, and with a closer look, can help scholars to understand Kongo urban design, building techniques, and town activities.

As we have seen through the works of the theorists cited above, and through these two European maps of Africa, cartography as a discipline shows us part of the history of the culture, the nations, possessions, and conquests. But it also shows us a peculiar form of communication. The theory of cartography demonstrates the impossibility of summarizing and generalizing about a discipline that is formed by a diversity of styles and forms with their own historical, political, and cultural demands, and a long history and historiography. In the case of Africa, cartography has the challenge of putting into practice all of the history of the earlier cartography as well as to create new forms of understanding mapmaking as a language. Finally, cartography could be, in the case of Africa, a medium of intercommunication between Europe and Africa, a back-and-forth between the politics, the desire to represent the other in its differences through art.

The cartographic representation is a form between painting, engraving and drawing that, like such media, uses representational language to convey a form of cultural history of the peoples portrayed as well as the domination of the colonizer over the colonized, that which represents over that which is represented.

SORROW IN THE TROPICS AND REVISING PRIMARY SOURCES

What I refer to as politics by other means relates to the existing tension recognized in landscape painting theory between two modes of representation: the "sublime" and the "picturesque." Generally speaking, pictorial representation and conceptual indebtedness share the same object of study in representing the visual knowledge of nature as place and space. The notion of the sublime is generally used in the context of American and European artistic practices and theorized in association with a particular socioeconomic formation in the eighteenth and nineteenth centuries of well-established colonial powers (European) or in an emerging power like the United States in the late nineteenth century. The notion of the sublime is used in case studies of Latin American and Caribbean landscape painting as an adjective to describe a subject matter, not as a manner of representation. In Cuban art, historical studies are known as *costumbrismo*, a concept explained by Ernesto Cardet Villegas, in his essay "Discovering the Cuban Landscape." Villegas wrote, "The portrayal of local customs as a subject was adopted later in painting than in lithography; nevertheless, it reached artistic excellence. Like prints, the genre provided information on the customs and settings ofCuban society at the time."[27]

The challenge here is how to explain why visual content in the sublime and picturesque (as *costumbrismo*) have been given such distinct theoretical formulations even though they share the same visual principles and subject matter. Instead of highlighting this common ground, art history discourse discerns between the sublime and picturesque as different styles and attaches different moral values to each of them.

Both pictorial models convey knowledge on which the perception of nature as place and space depends, but the purportedly vital distinction made between both appears to be solely based on how knowledge varied across time and space in America, Europe, Latin America, and the Caribbean and how such a differential is associated with each specific pictorial style. Both types indicate a desire to know nature in an attempt to understand its meaning through various ideologies such as religion, in which questions of moral archetype and

27 Angela L. Miller, Janet C. Barlo, Bryan J. Wolf and Jenifer L. Roberts. *American Encounter: Art, History and Cultural Identity.* Upper Saddle River, NJ: Pearson Education, Inc., 2008.

moral lessons are critical, like the belief that God is nature or nature is a manifestation of God. Furthermore, both representations reflect the apolitics of economic expansion in the nineteenth century, particularly the American growth to the west coast and its taming of the "Wild West," which included a policy of conservation that promoted supporting the natural environment by implementing the tourist scheme and creating national parks and nature reserves. In other words, the sublime and picturesque are pictorial orders that reflect ideology, beliefs and politics—visual schemas that provide psychological access to content and facilitate the processing and framing of a sociocultural mindset.

Comparing Thomas Cole's painting *The Expulsion of Paradise* with Esteban Chartrand's paintings *Cimarrón* and *El Valle de Yumurí* illustrates how, contrary to art history historiography, the sublime and picturesque work with the same aesthetic and conceptual principles. Both artists work with the convention of the beautiful by facilitating a visual narrative guided by compositional elements such as symmetry, balance, and harmony (see figures 16 – 18). Thomas Cole represents the contrast between the pre-industrial time (primeval) and the industrial revolution; Esteban Chartrand represents that between the economy of the plantation, in which the economy of slavery signifies an industrial setting and space of production and labor and the representation o f self-liberated Africans in a pristine (primeval) landscape.

Thomas Cole's picture evokes the idea of gratitude, forgiveness and favor versus the disruption of the steady rhythms of an industrial landscape. He brings his personal experience with the industrial revolution, loss and displacement in his own household. Esteban Chartrand believed, like Thomas Cole, in a "higher style of landscape, in service of social criticism," a way to imbue the landscape with "moral and imaginative power," and viewed the depiction of a landscape as an imaginative leap into those "invisible" meanings that lie unseen on the other side of nature. For Cole, this was visually conjuring the sense of turbulence versus paradise; for Chartrand, the rain forest is a safe place containing controlled chaos, freedom, and an entitlement to liberty, unlike the order of the valley plantation and its system of slavery and industrialization.

In Esteban Chartrand's painting, the pictorial space is organized in a dichotomy of light on the right side of the composition versus darkness on the left side of the painting, the reverse of Thomas Cole's placement of the lightness of paradise on the right and the darkness, evocative of his personal loss, on the left. In the two pieces, the relationship between clarity and darkness occurs through a diagonal; the clarity is placed in the upper part of the pictorial space. Esteban Chartrand strategically inverts the use of this visual resource, altering the place where the idea of clarity is located in the composition, as compared to Cole. Chartrand represents the plantation as a symbol of slavery and of the attendant alienation of the human subject (Africans), and uses the uninterrupted smoke coming out of the chimneys of the visible large-size sugar mills scattered through the valley, rendered as if the wind was blowing in the opposite direction of darkness, to visually suggest the idea of freedom and self-liberation.

Esteban Chartrand suggests that the idea of self-liberation, auto-determination and safety are closely connected instead of choosing to represent the African subjects without agencies, as passive actors in history. Chartrand expressed these ideas in depicting a group scene, insisting on distinguishing several of the psychological features of each character. The first in the painting can be seen as a character who appears to be relaxed, walking from a cave-like entry point to a cave toward the front to join the rest of the group, echoing the title of the painting and other symbolic aids deployed in the picture. A cave in the popular imagination is associated with a place to take refuge or hide. It is also a standard reference for a home for initiation and religious importance to perform rituals strongly related

Figure 16. Thomas Cole. Expulsion from the Garden of Eden, 1828.

Figure 17. Esteban Chartrand. The Runaways, 1880.

to the four most critical Afro-Cuban religions. Finally, two characters to the left of the composition appear relaxed, in a thoughtful mode, like they are contemplating the landscape (future) to come as a new time of freedom. The tradition of representing the African as the subject of violence, passive actors or "empty hands and heads" is exemplified in the artwork of a few nineteenth-century artists, including Víctor Patricio Landaluze *Cimarrón Luchando con Perros Cazadores* (Runaway Slave Fighting the Hunting Dogs), ca.

Figure 18. Esteban Chartrand Valle del Yumurí (*Yumurí Valley*), ca. 1875.

1860s and *The Cane Harvest*, 1874., and Esteban Chartrand's painting *View of then Tinguaro Sugar Mill, No. 1 -Boiler House*, 1874.

Colonial status, independence, nation-building, cultural revival and racial divisions are essential notions to be considered as marking a period of transformation in the postcolonial Caribbean. The research will focus on how these broad, central concepts translate into a visual inquiry, paying particular attention to economic, cultural and political specificities and how African and indigenous cultures have contributed to modern art practices in the Caribbean. I will examine the work of well-known Caribbean Avant-garde and modern artists through the lens of contemporary theory and investigate late fifteenth to late nineteenth-century historical visual continuities and visual culture. Whereas Caribbean modern art has traditionally been encompassed by Latin American modern art theory, the proposed research will initiate a critical dialogue about the formulation of notions, including Avant-garde, modernism and modernity in the Caribbean as distinct from, yet with parallels to, Latin America. Reformulating the "modern" experience in Caribbean art will also involve considering how to judge in contrast to the historical formulation of European Avant-garde and modernity theories (see figure 19).

I intend to provide a critical framework that distinguishes between modernity as a historical stage, modernization as a social process that attempts to construct modernity, and modernism as a cultural project that takes place at several points during the development of capitalism. Rather than speculate about or assume a default trajectory for a Caribbean artistic experience into the art history theories known as Avant-garde and modernism, I will question the assumption of the existing theoretical approach that it is possible to promote cultural modernism. At the same time, socioeconomic modernization is so uneven, one has to examine whether the measurement of Caribbean modernity should diverge from an idealized vision of how this process happened in Europe.

MODERN PRELUDE

In Cuba, from the 1930s on, cultural production became more independent. At the start of the second half of the twentieth century, social science, art and literature elites saw clear signs of socioeconomic modernization in Cuba and the wider Caribbean. The growth of higher education, artistic programs and literary markets driven by these socioeconomic changes helped to professionalize cultural life. The gap between cultured and popular was no longer defined in terms of social class, as the division between an educated elite and an illiterate or semi-literate majority. High culture became the domain of a small faction within the bourgeoisie and middle classes, while most upper and middle classes became subject instead to the mass programming of the cultural industry.

Endorsing the argument against the view that Avant-garde art theory in Cuba played a vindicating role in representing African people is insufficient. We need, additionally, a discussion to show that historically African people are perceived and portrayed as symbolic of the naïve gaze,

Figure 19. Eduardo Abela, The Triumph of the Rumba, ca. 1928.

objects of curiosity and exploitation.

Eduardo Abela is an example of changes in traditional patterns of exoticism. African people as depicted in Abela's painting *The Triumph of the Rumba* are not vindicated by misfortune, a lack of artistic representation or recognition of their intellectual contributions to art history discourses. Africa as a subject matter in Abela's painting shifted from a rigid pseudo-political argument that denied other aspects of social and human complexity, to one referencing African people's art, culture and religion as critical to the formation of Cuban identity.

Abela's image is cleverly centered around African music and dance, indicating a coming out and marking its presence to the spectators in a manner that suggests it is emblematic of Cuban identity, or at least a newly renegotiated identity that has the opportunity to be more inclusive. Artists make choices not just about how to represent a subject or the theme itself, but also how to position the subject or theme in a specific moment in history. Abela visually argues not just that African culture should be a theme within the conceptual frame of the Avant-garde, but also that such framing is aesthetically pertinent and necessary. This positioning of a cultural form (Rumba) and the people who performed it (African descendants) as the central proposition, an archetype of Cuban ethnogenesis depicts it as a building block of Cuban national identity and primordial cultural heritage. Abela paints a sonic and kinetic event, representing Rumba in a way not previously done and suggesting the complexity inherent in its encompassing of dance, lyrics, music and social and religious commentaries. The kinetic aestheticism, or representation of time and movement, of the piece has links to the futuristic art of Filippo Tommasso Marinetti's *Blue Dancer* of 1912 and Marcel Duchamp's *Nude Descending a Staircase, No. 2* of 1912, and its utilization was formative in the debate around Cuban culture today.

Abela also incorporates as emblematic of the Cuban nation a conveniently placed female figure. This symbol conveys ideas associated with Cuban national identity and its "syncretic" nature. Abela visually alludes to the notion of syncretism through his representation of a woman portraying specific principles and moral values identified with the Yoruba religion in Cuba. Here, she emerges from the sea as Yemaya, the goddess of the sea in the Yoruba Lucumi religion, syncretized with the Catholic virgin "Our Lady of Cobre," the patroness of Cuba. The frontal approach challenges the audience, forcing, along with drums, dancers, and a banana tree, a recognition of complex dual identities.

Abela's work is forward looking and represents the beginning

Figure 20. Roberto Diago Querol. Untitled, 1944.

of a new way to create and consider Caribbean art, posing the critical question of what such a field might mean in the twenty-first century and what the historical archive can convey regarding an artist of this early Avant-garde and modern moment (see figure 20).

Perhaps the most daring work of Cuban artists comprising the second generation of Avant-garde is that of Roberto Diago Querol, whose importance is comparable to that of Eduardo Abela in the first generation. Querol strategically proposes an Afro-Cuban theme while working within the canonized genre of "still life" in Western art. Querol takes a multi-referential approach to the still life, one directly linked both to the history of the genre in Western art and to vernacular domestic life in Cuba. Querol capitalized on the meaning and representation of floral arrangements widespread in domestic spaces in Cuba, both in the countryside and the city, and across all sectors of society, from peasants to workers, to the bourgeoisie. Floral arrangements are also one of the most common religious performances in all Afro-Cuban traditions and in all the branches of spiritism that are currently practiced in Cuba. The double meanings and ambiguity noticeable in the painting's intermediate representation of the flower bucket suggests that Diago Querol is fully aware of the notion of syncretism and transculturation introduced by Fernando Ortiz in 1940s, especially in his publication, *Cuban Counterpoint: Tobacco and Sugar*.

Exploration of the tradition of the floral arrangement was a popular subject for many of the Cuban artists in the Avant-garde and modern art periods, but Diago Querol goes further than most in interrogating its layered meanings. Here, Querol depicts as a central theme a flower arrangement made of twelve white roses. Floral offerings in Afro-Cuban religions are usually twelve flowers or roses without thorns, with a powerful taboo related to the number of flowers, roses and thorns, whereby, for example, an arrangement of fewer than twelve elements or one with thorns automatically nullifies the intention of the offering. Diago suggestively designs the leaves of the flowers with simple outlines as sketches very similar to the use of line-like motifs widespread in individual symbols comprising a graphic writing system known as *firmas* and used in Cuba within the Kongo-based religion *Palo Monte.* A second Afro-Cuban conceptual element is noticeable in Querol's design of the floor tiles. In this example, the tiles have the fluidity typical in the graphic rules followed to create and bring together various meanings in the *Palo Monte firmas.* Diago Querol isolates multiple functional motifs, known as seals, which function as a building block of graphic writing and converts them into independent symbols without an apparent intention to articulate any idea or express something.

One of the characteristics of postmodernism is the breaking down of divisions between the erudite and the popular. One can no longer rigidly associate social class with cultural status, and neither can this status be linked to a fixed repertoire of symbolic goods. How, politically and culturally, we used to associate "popular" with "national" in the 1960s and 1970s is no longer valid. A shift toward the international-popular occurred during the 1980s, beginning with the Havana and São Paulo Biennales when popular culture looked outward from its original territory to communicate and interact with other players in the elite global art scene. The attention to popular culture became the cause for an ideologically and politically charged theme, which was increasingly reflected in artistic practices and capitalized on an assumed common history among all Caribbean nations. Arguably the first space where such an exchange of cultural paradigms materialized, Cuba is an ideal location to consider the relationship between mass and popular culture and high art on a global scale. Most often conflated with the mass culture in the industrialized West, the popular culture within Cuba remains an elusive and open term. Uneven economic development, varying education and media access levels, national appropriation of indigenous and folk cultures, political and artistic movements under authoritarian regimes, and a diverse mixture of European, African, Asian and indigenous cultural influences contribute to the term's pluralism in this regional context. I would broadly define popular culture in Cuba as a spectrum of artistic practices outside the institutionalized and canonized forms of knowledge and aesthetic production generally defined as "high" culture. Also, an argument can be made that it comprises what has been described, often derogatorily, as folk culture, mass culture, and political or activist art. Although frequently juxtaposed with the implicitly superior "fine art," there is a need to examine how these forms have been culturally and visually influential for other artistic and social spheres.

The absence of a satisfactory approach to the contemporary study of Cuban art has not prevented contemporary artists in Cuba from creating robust responses to and extensions of Cuban visual and cultural practices. Although celebrating contemporary Cuban art to the exclusion of a more nuanced study of other artistic practices with longer histories is problematic, the work of many contemporary artists could inform modern discourse about Cuban art. Their work, and the increasingly global art scene in which it is produced and consumed, enables the exploration of how Cuban principles are taken up, extended and reinterpreted by artists in a new cultural paradigm. I intend to further examine how these artists attempt to bridge the perceived gap between art and cultureby intertwining Western and non-Western visual practices and melding concepts of "modernity" with traditional elements. In some cases, offering new interpretations of archetypal images, contemporary Cuban-influenced work also reveals the pervasiveness of certain Western conceptual memes. It highlights the difficulty in exploring Cuban art on its own terms.

BIBLIOGRAPHY

Adams, Monni. "African Visual Arts from an Art Historical Perspective." *African Studies Review* 32, no. 2 (1989).

------------------. "African Art Studies: The State of the Discipline." Washington D.C., 1987.

Angela L. Miller, Janet C. Barlo, Bryan J. Wolf and Jenifer L. Roberts. *American Encounter: Art, History and Cultural Identity.* Upper Saddle River, NJ: Pearson Education, Inc., 2008.

Bascom, William. *African Art in Cultural Perspective: An Introduction.* New York: W. W. Norton, 1973.

Battestini, Simon. *African Writing and Text.* New York-Ottawa-Toronto: Legas, 2000.

Beier, Uli. *Contemporary Art in Africa.* F.A. Praeger, 1968.

Blier, Suzanne Preston. "Words about Words about Icons: Iconologology and the Study of African Art." *Art Journal* 47, No. 2 (Summer 1988): 75-87.

Bentley, W. Holman. *Dictionary and Grammar of the Kongo Language.* London: Trubner & CO, 1887.

------------------------. *Appendix to the Dictionary and Grammar of the Kongo Language.* London: Trubner & CO, 1895.

Bondil, Nathalie., and Tim. Bernard. *Cuba: Art and History, from 1868 to Today.* Montréal: Montreal Museum of Fine Arts, 2008.

Bunseki Lumanisa, A. Fu-Kiau kia. *N'kongo ye Nza Yakun'zungidila. Le Mukongo et le Monde qui l'Entourait,* Zamenga Batukezanga, (Kinshasa: Office Nationale de la Recherche et de Développement, 1969).

Cabrera, Lydia. *El Monte: Igbo Fina Ewe Orisha, Vititinfinda.* Havana: Ediciones C.R., 1954.

--------------------. *Vocabulario Congo: El Bantu que se Habla en Cuba.* Chicherekú: Miami, 1984.

Castellanos, Jorge, and Isabel Castellanos. *Cultura Afrocubana, 4 vols.* Miami: Ediciones Universal, 1988.

Cavazzi, Giovani Antonio da Montecuccolo. *Istorica descrizione de' tre regni Congo: Matamba ed Angola, 2 Vols*. Bologna: Giacomo Monti, 1687.

Cole, Herbert. *African Arts of Transformation*. Santa Barbara: The Art Galleries of the University of California, Santa Barbara, 1970.

Collins, Robert and Ruth Iyob. *Problems in African History*. Princeton, New Jersey: Markus Wiener Publishers, 2013.

Crowley, Daniel J. "Traditional and Contemporary Art in Africa." In *Expanding Horizons in African Studies*, edited by Gewndolen M. Carter and Ann Paden. Evanston: Northwestern University Press, 1969.

Curnow, Kathy. *The Bright Continent: African Art History*. Cleveland, OH: MSL Academic Endeavors Imprint of Michael Schwartz Library at Cleveland State University, 2021.

Danto, Arthur C., ed. *Art/Artifact: African Art in Anthropology Collections*. New York: Munich: Center for African Art; Prestel Verlag, 1988.

Drewal, Henry, John Pemberton, Rowland Abiodun and Allen Wardell., eds. *Yoruba: Nine Centuries of African Art and Thought*. Center for African Art in Association with H.N. Abrams, 1989.

Faïk-Nzuji, Clementine M. *Tracing Memory*. Quebec: Canadian Museum of Civilization, 1996.

Fagg, William. "In Search of Meaning in African Art." In *Primitive Art and Society.* London & New York: Oxford University Press, 1973.

Fuente, Alejandro de la, ed. *Grupo Antillano: the art of Afro-Cuba = el arte de Afro-Cuba.* Trans. Julia Romero and Tom Holloway. Santiago de Cuba: Fundación Caguayo, 2013.

Frobenius, Leo. *Und Afrika Sprach: Auf den Trümmern des klassischen Atlantis.* Berlin: Vita, 1912.

Förster, Till and Sidney Littlefield Kasfir, eds. *African Art and Agency in the Workshop.* Bloomington: Indiana University Press, 2013.

Gabay, Clive. *Imagining Africa: Whiteness and the Western Gaze.* Cambridge University Press, 2018.

Galpin, Amy, Katherine Manthorne, and Jorge Duany. *In the Mind's Eye: Landscapes of Cuba = La Mirada de Quien Contempla: Paisajes de Cuba.* Lewes: Giles, 2022.

Gutiérrez, Lucinda., Ana Isabel. Moreno, and Patricia. Rubio Ornelas. *La revista Orígenes y la vanguardia cubana.* Madrid: D.G.E. Ediciones, 2000.

Hallen, Berry. Yoruba Moral Epistemology. In Kwasi Wiredu, ed. A Companion to African Philosophy. Malden, Massachusetts - Oxford, United Kingdom: Blackwell, 2004.

Hartman, Joseph R. "Race, Gender, Giants: Consensus and Dissensus in Cuban Cultural Politics." *Cultural politics (Biggleswade, England)* 14.2 (2018).

Hegel, G.W.F. *The Philosophy of History*, trans. J. Sibree, introduction C.J. Friedrich. New York: Dover Publications, 1956.

Eglash, Ron. *African Fractal: Modern Computing and Indigenous Design.* New Jersey-London: Rutgers University Press, 1999.

Emerling, Jae. Theory for Art History. Oxford: Routledge, 2005.

La Ilustración Española. Año XIX, No. XXX (15 de Agosto, 1875).

Libby, Gary Russell. *Two Centuries of Cuban Art, 1759-1959: From the Cuban Foundation Collection of the Museum of Arts and Sciences, Daytona Beach, Florida, and Additional Works from the Solomon R. Guggenheim Museum, New York, the Museum of Modern Art, New York, and the Museum of Modern Art of Latin America, Washington D.C.* Sarasota, Florida: John and Mable Ringling Museum of Art, 1980.

Martínez Ruiz, Bárbaro. In *Embodiments: Masterworks of African Figurative Sculpture. Munich: Prestel, 2015.*

----------------------------. "Mambo Comes from the Soul" in *Call and Response: Journeys in African Art*. New Haven: Yale University Gallery Press, 2000.

----------------------------. "Ma kisi Nsi: L'art de habitants de region de Mbanza Kongo" in *Angola figures de pouvoir*. Paris: Dapper Museum Press, 2010.

Juan Martínez *Cuban Art & National Identity; The Vanguardia Painters 1928-1950*. Gainesville: University Press of Florida, 1994.

Mbembe, Achille. *On the Postcolony.* Trans. Berkeley: University of California Press, 2001.

Meier, Prita. "Modernism in Africanist Art History: The Making of a New Discipline." In *The Modernist World*, edited by Stephen Ross and Allana C. Lindgren, 214–23. New York, NY: Routledge, 2015.

Mudimbe, V. Y. *The Invention of Africa: Gnosis, Philosophy, and the Order of Knowledge*. Bloomington and Indianapolis: Indiana University Press, 1988.

Oguibe, Olu. *Reading the Contemporary: African Art from Theory to the Marketplace*. London: Institute of International Visual Arts, 1999.

Okeke-Agulu, Chika. *Postcolonial Modernism: Art and Decolonization in Twentieth-Century Nigeria*, 2015.

Phillips, Tom. *Africa: The Art of a Continent*. London; Munich; New York: Royal Academy of Arts; Prestel, 1995.

Pivin, Jean Loup and N'gone Fall, eds. *An Anthology of African Art: The Twentieth Century*. New York: Distributed Art Publishers, 2002.

Price, Sally. "Cultures in Dialogue?" in *Anthropology of the Arts: A Reader*, edited by Gretchen Bakke and Marina Peterson, 313-318. London & New York: Bloomsbury Academic, an imprint of Bloomsbury Publishing, 2017.

Quarcoopome, Nii O. and Veit Arlt, eds. *Through African Eyes: The European in African Art, 1500 to Present*. Detroit: Detroit Institute of Arts, 2009.

Roberts, Mary Nooter. "Tradition Is Always Now: African Arts and the Curatorial Turn." *African Arts* 45, no. 1 (2012): 1–7.

------------------------. *Secrecy: African Art That Conceals and Reveals*. New York: Museum for African Art, 1993.

Sieber, Roy. "Invention and Reinvention in the Traditional Arts." *African Arts* 28, no. 2 (Spring 1995): 24-33, 90.

----------. "The Aesthetic of Traditional African Art." In *Art and Aesthetics in Primitive Societies*, by Carol F. Jopling, ed. New York: E. P. Dutton, 1971.

Sieber, Roy and Roslyn A. Walker. *African Art in the Cycle of Life*. Washington, D.C.: Published for the National Museum of African Art by the Smithsonian Press, 1987.

Sippial, Tiffany. "Afro-Cuban Religious Arts: Popular Expressions of Cultural Inheritance in Espiritismo and Santería. By KristineJuncker. Gainesville: University Press of Florida, 2014, p. 216, $74.95." *The Latin Americanist (Orlando, Fla.)* 58.4 (2014).

Taiwo, Olufemi. http://www.virginia.edu/woodson/courses/aas102%20 (spring%2001)/articles/femi.htm

Thompson, Robert Farris. *African Art in Motion: Icon and Act.* Los Angeles: University of California Press, 1974.

--------------------------------. *The Four Moments of the Sun*. Washington D.C.: National Gallery of Art, 1981.

-------------------------------. *Flash of the Spirit: Afro-American Art & Philosophy*. New York: Vintage, 1984.

Thornton, John. *The Kingdom of Kongo: Civil War and Transformation 1641-1718*. Madison: The University of Wisconsin Press, 1983.
--------------------. *African and Africans in Making of the Atlantic World, 1400-1800*. New York: Cambridge University, 1998.

Tsang, Martin A. "How Afro-Cuban Beaded Art Reflects Religion, Heritage, and Anthropology." *Chiricú* 2.1 (2017).

Vansina, Jan. *Art history in Africa: An Introduction to Method*. London: New York, 1984.

Visonà, Monica Blackmun, Robin Poynor, et al. *A history of art in Africa*. London: Laurence King Publishing Ltd., 2008.

Vogel, Susan. "Whither African Art? Emerging Scholarship at the End of an Age." *African Arts* 38, no. 4 (December 1, 2005): 12–91.

----------------. *Art/artifact; African Art in Anthropology Collections*. N.Y.: Museum for African Art, 1995.

Wiredu, Kwasi, ed. A Companion to African Philosophy. Malden, Massachusetts - Oxford, United Kingdon: Blackwell, 2004.

Young, Robert. *White Mythologies: Writing History and the West*. 2nd ed. London; New York: Routledge, 2004.

Zaslavsky, Claudia. *Africa Counts: Number and Pattern in African Cultures*. 3rd ed. Chicago, Ill: Lawrence Hill Books, 1999.

Zuberi, Tukufu, and Eduardo Bonilla-Silva, eds. *White Logic, White Methods: Racism and Methodology*. Lanham: Rowman & Littlefield Publishers, 2008.